everyday
SOUS VIDE
it's all french to me

Copyright © 2018 by Chelsea Cole
Photographs copyright © 2018 by Chelsea Cole and Carly Jayne

All rights reserved.
Published and printed in the United States of America. No part of this book may be used or reproduced in any manner whatsoever without written permission except in the case of brief quotations embodied in articles and reviews.

For more information, please contact Chelsea Cole at chelsea@aducksoven.com.

ISBN 978-0-9980499-0-8
Ebook ISBN 978-0-9980499-1-5

Book design by Carly Jayne.
Food photography by Chelsea Cole.
Portrait photography by Carly Jayne.

www.aducksoven.com

Cook Like a Goldfish
in a small bowl of water
CHELSEA COLE
SOUS VIDE
a hot tub for meats
CHELSEA COLE
You've got a need:
A NEED FOR VIDE
CHELSEA COLE
A Toy Named Sous
CHELSEA COLE
SOUS MANY MOUTHS TO FEED
CHELSEA COLE
Get Vide up From the Feet Up
CHELSEA COLE
Get Your Feet Wet Getting Your Meat Wet
CHELSEA COLE
H2-Oh Yeah!
Sous Vide Cooking
CHELSEA COLE
In a Wada da Vida
CHELSEA COLE
SOUS YOU THINK YOU CAN VIDE?
CHELSEA COLE
SOUS ME!
SOUS VIDE COOKING
CHELSEA COLE
Wet, Hot,
CULINARY SUMMER
CHELSEA COLE

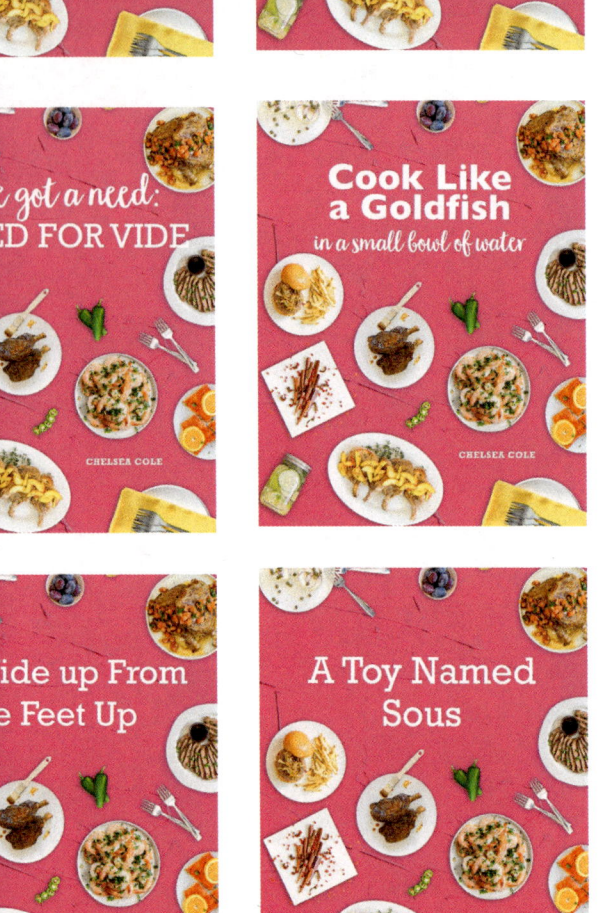

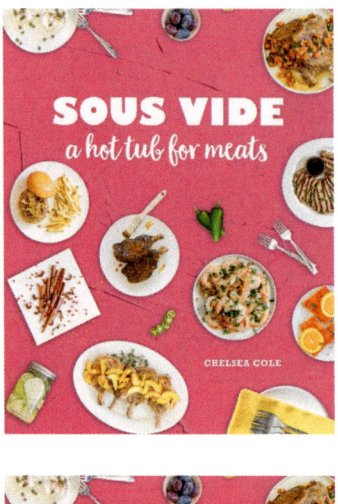

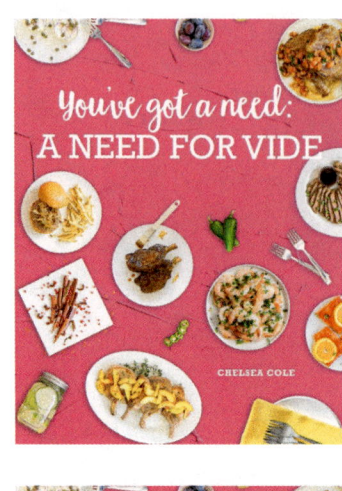

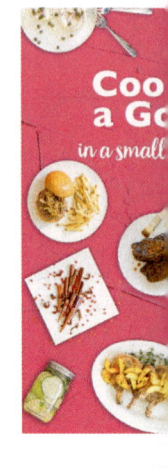

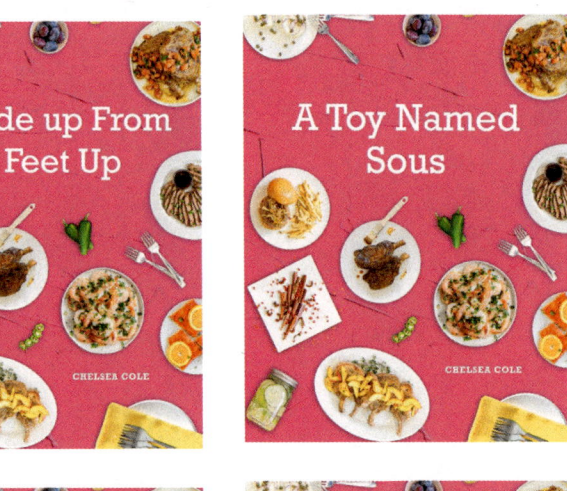

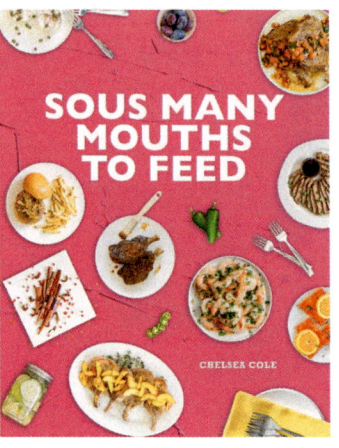

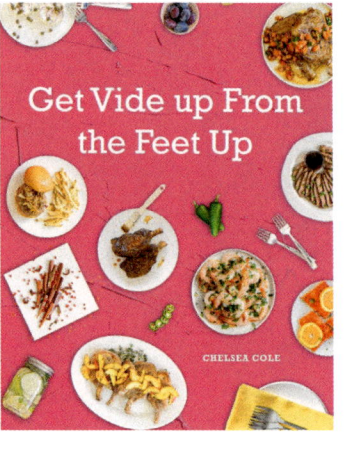

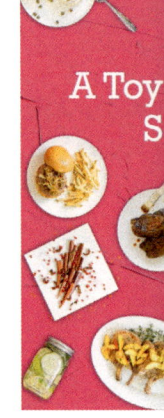

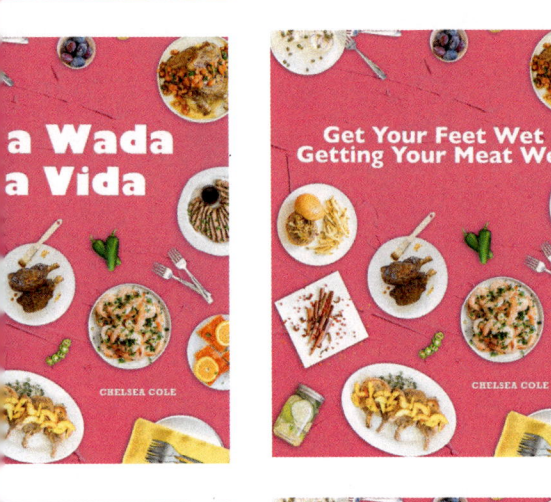

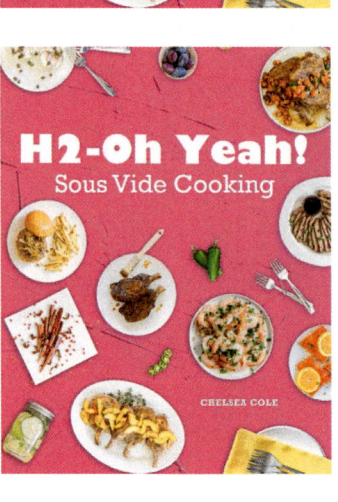

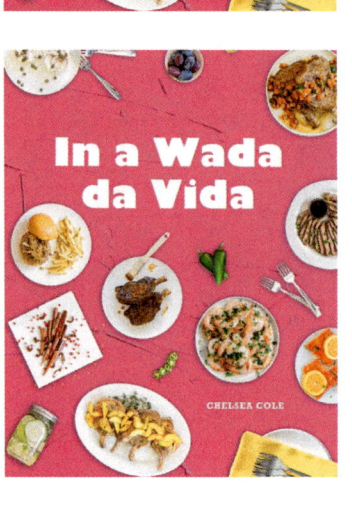

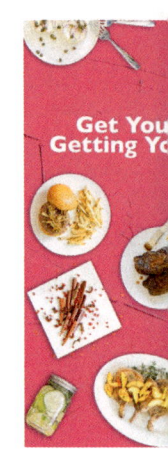

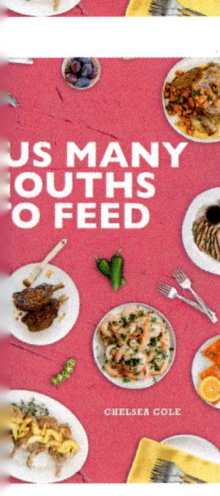

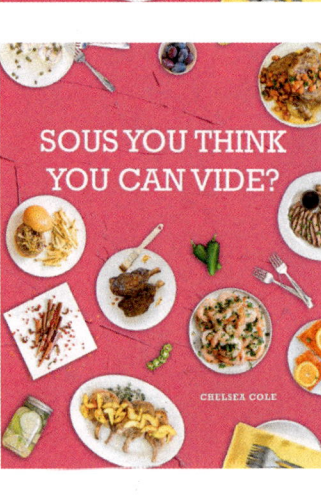

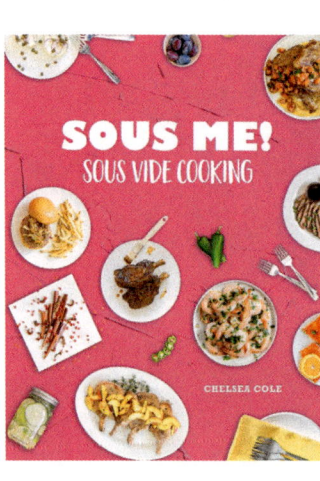

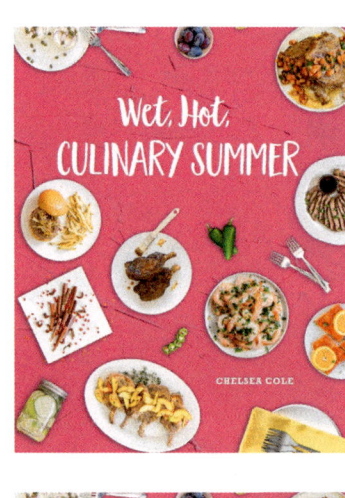

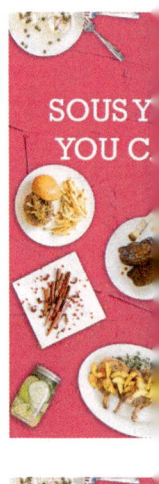

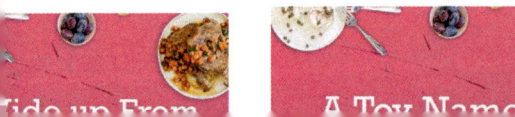

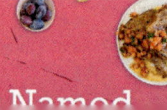

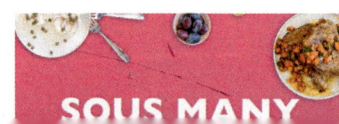

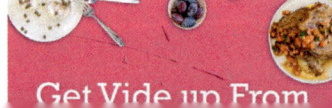

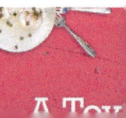

TABLE OF CONTENTS

Introduction...	6
Sous Vide: Why Tho?..	8
Sous Vide 101...	9
Better-than-Starbucks Egg Bites...........................	12
Overnight Oats (But t*oat*ally Warm and Yummy).......	22
The Quickest Pickles...	32
Not Your Mom's Pork Chops.................................	42
So Perfect I'll Steak My Life On It.........................	52
Shrimpossible to Mess Up.....................................	62
Salmon to be Excited About..................................	72
White Fish: The Other Other White Meat................	82
Stuffed Burgers To Stuff Your Face With.................	92
Mash It Like You Mean It......................................	102
Dessert Oasis...	112
Liquor Infusions: My Boozy Brainchild....................	120
Acknowledgments...	130
Index..	132

<---

Alternative titles provided by Chelsea's husband, Eric

THE AUTHOR: IT'S ME!

Hi. Welcome to my book. This book is special, because it's my very first (and I hope there are more).

The short of it: I'm from Portland, Oregon (born and raised - don't @ me, bro) and at the time of this publication I am in my late twenties. I went to the University of Oregon and am a big football fan ('Sco Ducks!). By day, I do digital marketing for small businesses, but I've been food blogging since before it was cool (2010) and it makes my heart sing. I'm one of those odd people that's married to her high school sweetheart. He's a high school teacher and a master of puns.

I spend most of my free time in the kitchen. Cooking became my stress outlet in college, and remains that today. Instead of using it to tune out the pressure of school work and my part time job, it now serves as my way to unwind from a long day at work while my husband sits at the bar and we debrief about each others' days while having a beer. It's my favorite.

Wanna stalk me?
Blog: aducksoven.com
Instagram: @aducksoven

MY SOUS VIDE LOVE STORY

Let me set the scene: it's August 2017. Per tradition, I've dragged my husband and parents to a trendy restaurant in Portland, Oregon that I usually wouldn't go to because money but it's my birthday, and mom and dad want to treat.

Despite the fact that they're footing the bill for dinner, they've brought gifts. After we get our drinks and place our order, I open them: a new top, gorgeous jewelry. Then I get to the last big box and unwrap a new kitchen gadget. This kitchen gadget was one I'd seen around and been curious about, but was a little wary of approaching. It seemed scary and pretentious. Even so, I'd always wondered, and I'd drifted to and away from it during many an online shopping trip.

Thank god my mom forced an introduction, because this gadget upped my cooking game in a way I didn't know was possible!

SOUS VIDE: why tho?

Right here, right now, it's time to get over the idea that sous vide cooking is some Frenchie, stuffy, totally nerdy way of cooking. It IS those things, yes, but it's not JUST those things. Thanks to new, inexpensive immersion circulators, it's an approachable way to take a ton of the stress out of cooking dishes you'd otherwise try to stay away from.

First things first, let's make sure you can **pronounce** sous vide #noshame. Ready? Soo (like "moo" with an s) veed. Go forth and sound like a pro.

Now, **what is it?** Sous vide is a cooking method where you put your food in a plastic bag or glass jar and place it in a water bath at a specific temperature. The water bath stays at that specific temperature, usually for a longer period of time than you'd normally cook that food. Got it? Food in bag, bag in bath, leave it there for a while.

The next question for us to tackle: **why is this something you'd want to do?** We're going to use steak as our example food in this explanation, but this logic applies to all food. The doneness of steak is related to the temperature the center of the steak reaches. So, the center of a rare steak is literally colder than the center of a well-done steak. Right? Right. Using an immersion circulator, you can keep a water bath at exactly whatever temperature you'd like. I like a medium-rare steak, so I cook steak at 129 degrees F. When I place a bag of steak in a water bath set to this temperature, it never gets any hotter than 129 degrees F. I could cook that steak for days and it would still be rare, because it's all about temperature. When it's done cooking in the water bath, it gets a quick sear in a screaming hot pan, and that's it. You can't overcook it, no matter how long you cook it #mindblown.

Sous vide is also wonderful because you can get a tougher cut of meat and cook it long enough to tenderize it, while still keeping it medium. For our squeamish people, you can pasteurize a medium steak, while still keeping that lovely texture. No more well-done steaks for our germaphobes (I'm looking at you, father-in-law). Cooking for a crowd? You can prep several servings at once, get the main dish done hours in advance, then just sear to serve.

What else can this magic machine do? Make the silkiest, dreamiest sous vide egg bites; crank out perfect creme brulee with only blending as the prep work; simmer oatmeal while you sleep; prep the most luscious mashed potatoes; and pickle in just 2 hours flat. "Why haven't I been doing this for always?!" is the question you should be asking yourself right now.

WHAT YOU NEED

For links to specific product suggestions, head to my blog! **aducksoven.com**

Most importantly, you need an **immersion circulator**. This is a device that you place into a water bath to circulate the water and keep it at a certain temperature. Think of it as the machine that makes a hot tub a hot tub instead of a mini pool. There are lots out there, and I've heard good things about many of them. My personal favorites come from Vesta Precision out of Seattle. Check out the reviews and features and snag the one that seems best for how you want to use it. I will say: the wifi ones are fun because before going to work, you can put your food in an ice bath, then turn on the circulator remotely when you're ready to start cooking. Pretty neat.

Next up, you're going to need **bags** to cook your food in. Although they can be a little more expensive, I recommend using a vacuum sealer and vacuum seal bags. I also recommend Vesta Precision for these. You can also just use a heavy duty zipper-top bag. Finally, there are reusable, BPA-free vac-pac bags. They come with a little pump to suck all the air out of your bags. The downside: they're annoying to clean and don't make it through many uses.

So, what should you use to **contain your water bath**? You can use whatever you want. A stock pot, dutch oven, any kind of big container. Some people even use coolers so they can do a whole buncha food at once. I like to use what's called a "Cambro" which is the brand name for a large polycarbonate container used in restaurants for making large batches of food. These containers are awesome because they resist heat (don't absorb it and leak it out!), they're lightweight, and they're sturdy.

You'll also need **clips** of some kind (binder clips work just fine) to keep your bags from sinking all the way into the water bath - the seal needs to stay above the water, or water can get into the bag (unless you're using a vacuum sealer).

A **blow torch** comes in handy for caramelizing and giving color to some of your dishes. A few recipes in this book require a blowtorch (like creme brulee!). And let's be real: it's fun to play with fire.

I recommend a **blender** for a lot of the recipes in here, but it certainly doesn't need to be a fancy high powered one, and worst case scenario, use a whisk. NBD.

I call for **ghee** as my cooking oil of choice throughout this book. Why, you ask? We need to sear at super high heat to just give the outside of the meat some color. Ghee has a really high smoke point and can withstand these crazy temps. If you prefer a different cooking oil that can take the heat, feel free to sub ghee out for that.

GETTING RID OF THE AIR

The key to sous viding successfully (yes, it's a verb now) is removing all the air from your bags before adding them to your water bath. There are a few different ways to do that.

Use a vacuum sealer. This is the most sure-fire way to make sure all the air is truly removed. It works well with any recipes that don't have a lot of liquid.

Using the hand pump that comes with reusable bags. A little more work, but less expensive than using vacuum seal bags every time. This also only works with recipes that don't have a lot of liquid.

Water displacement method. For several of these recipes, you'll use the water displacement method to get the air out of your bag because they contain so much liquid. Here's how you do it: add all the ingredients to the bag according to the recipe's instructions. Zip the top of the bag until it's almost closed, but leave a little crack. Submerge the bag, starting from the bottom, in a large container of water (I recommend just using your water bath before you start heating it), until the water has just reached the zipper - do not submerge the zipper. Direct the air towards the crack in the zipper, then zip closed. Most of the air should be removed.

TIME DOESN'T MATTER
(but it also matters)

The great thing about sous vide cooking is that you're never going to be standing over a dish watching it like a hawk to make sure you don't overcook it or burn it or do something to wreck it. This type of carefree-cooking is something we've only gotten from slow cookers in days past. But that doesn't mean you should go crazy with the cooking times. This is the only time in the book that I'll get this technical, but it's for food safety reasons, you feel me?

The bacteria we're all afraid of dies at 130 degrees F. Cooking at temperatures less than 130 degrees F is essentially the same as letting food sit at room temperature, which is only safe for 3 hours or less (that's the time at which those nasty bacteria start forming). So, if you're like me and love a medium-rare steak, we don't want to cook it for more than 3 hours to stay in the safety zone.

Time also affects texture. The longer you cook something, the more it breaks the food down. So, be thoughtful about your timing, and know that I've been thoughtful about what I recommend in this book. Eggs and desserts? Pretty precise timing. Meat? You've got a range of a couple hours. Seafood? A little more touchy, but some flexibility.

The cool thing about the fact that time affects temperature? Say you get a great deal on a cut of meat that's considered "bad" because it's tough. You can cook it for 36 hours if you want to to tenderize the hell out of it, and still enjoy meat cooked to medium. It's not just destined to stew!

Egg Bites

There are few things better than sous vide egg bites. They're silky, flavor-packed and perfect to cook in big batches and keep in the fridge for heat-and-eat breakfasts all week. Yes, they're rich, but they average around 250 calories each, so they aren't the calorie bomb you'd expect.

All of these recipes have the same base: eggs and dairy. You can change up the dairy and play with the fillings, but I've included my favorite ways to prepare these bites. If you're looking for a way to avoid cow's milk, I'd recommend using cashew milk. Otherwise, please use full fat dairy and don't look back. Life is short.

Many sections in this book are going to include variations for time and temperature - this is not one of them. My suggestion: 185 degrees F for 30 minutes. You can go a little longer on the time if you need to, but that's the only variation I'd make. **DON'T BE A RULE BREAKER.** Be a rule follower. I'm watching you!

Looking to up your nutrient game? Throw a few cups of spinach into the blender for these bites. You won't taste a thing, and you'll get some greens in with your breakfast!

To reheat these guys, remove the lid and pop 'em in the microwave on high for 45 seconds - one minute.

Sun-Dried Tomato & Goat Cheese EGG BITES

The tanginess of goat cheese levels up these bites like you wouldn't believe, and sun-dried tomato is goat cheese's BFF. Spinach joins the party to make sure we behave ourselves… at least a little.

6 Servings

Ingredients
Cooking spray
8 eggs
1 cup heavy cream
2 tsp salt
½ tsp ground black pepper
1 tsp Italian seasoning (or your favorite unsalted dried herb blend)
2 cups spinach, chopped
½ cup goat cheese
¼ cup chopped sun-dried tomatoes

Directions
1. Get immersion circulator setup and start preheating water bath to 185 degrees F. This is a hot temperature for sous vide cooking: don't forget to place a trivet under your container!
2. Prepare 6 half pint sized jars, all should have undamaged lids. Remove lids and thoroughly spray interior with cooking spray.
3. Crack the eggs into the blender and add the heavy cream. Add the salt, pepper, and Italian seasoning to your blender and blend until completely combined, no individual white or yellow chunks.
4. Pour the egg mixture into prepared jars, dividing evenly between the jars.
5. Evenly distribute the spinach, goat cheese, and sun-dried tomatoes between the jars. Give each jar a small stir to just incorporate the ingredients.
6. Place the undamaged lids on your jars. Close to "finger tight" (you should be able to easily unscrew with just your fingertips). Drop jars carefully into water. Jars should be completely submerged and you should see small air bubbles escaping the jars. If the jars are floating, your lid is on too tight.
7. Let cook for 30 minutes. Remove from water bath and place on a towel. Let cool slightly before serving, or transfer to fridge once completely cooled.

Caramelized Onion & Brie EGG BITES

Feelin' extra this week? Plan on starting your mornings off by putting on your fancy pants. These caramelized onion and brie cheese egg bites take a little more effort than other egg bites, what with the caramelizing and all that, but they're so WORTH IT.

6 Servings

Ingredients
1 onion, cut into thin slices
½ tsp olive oil
Cooking spray
8 eggs
1 cup heavy cream
2 tsp salt
½ tsp ground black pepper
1 tsp Italian seasoning (or your favorite unsalted dried herb blend)
1/3 cup brie cheese cut into very small cubes

Directions
1. Get immersion circulator setup and start preheating water bath to 185 degrees F. This is a hot temperature for sous vide cooking: don't forget to place a trivet under your container!
2. Add the olive oil and onions to a medium-sized nonstick skillet over medium-low heat. Cook, stirring occasionally, until onions are soft and golden. This should take about 15 minutes. Set aside to cool.
3. Prepare 6 half pint sized jars, all should have undamaged lids. Remove lids and thoroughly spray interior with cooking spray.
4. Crack the eggs into the blender and add the heavy cream. Add the salt, pepper, and Italian seasoning to your blender and blend until completely combined, no individual white or yellow chunks.
5. Pour the egg mixture into prepared jars, dividing evenly between the jars.
6. Evenly distribute the onions and brie cheese between each jar. Give each jar a small stir to just incorporate the ingredients.
7. Place the undamaged lids on your jars. Close to "finger tight" (you should be able to easily unscrew with just your fingertips). Drop jars carefully into water. Jars should be completely submerged and you should see small air bubbles escaping the jars. If the jars are floating, your lid is on too tight.
8. Let cook for 30 minutes. Remove from water bath and place on a towel. Let cool slightly before serving, or transfer to fridge once completely cooled.

Cheddar, Bacon & Chive EGG BITES

This combo is a classic, a breakfast staple, the crowd pleaser of crowd pleasers. The scrambled eggs of your childhood, but silky smooth and decadent AF.

6 Servings

Ingredients
Cooking spray
8 eggs
1 cup heavy cream
2 tsp salt
½ tsp ground black pepper
1 tsp Italian seasoning (or your favorite unsalted dried herb blend)
6 slices of cooked bacon, torn into small pieces
½ cup shredded cheddar cheese
2 tbsp chopped chives

Directions
1. Get immersion circulator setup and start preheating water bath to 185 degrees F. This is a hot temperature for sous vide cooking: don't forget to place a trivet under your container!
2. Prepare 6 half pint sized jars, all should have undamaged lids. Remove lids and thoroughly spray interior with cooking spray.
3. Crack the eggs into the blender and add the heavy cream. Add the salt, pepper, and Italian seasoning to your blender and blend until completely combined, no individual white or yellow chunks.
4. Pour the egg mixture into prepared jars, dividing evenly between the jars.
5. Evenly distribute the shredded cheddar cheese and bacon between the jars. Give each jar a small stir to just incorporate the ingredients. Sprinkle the chives on the top of the mixture in each jar, evenly across the jars.
6. Place the undamaged lids on your jars. Close to "finger tight" (you should be able to easily unscrew with just your fingertips). Drop jars carefully into water. Jars should be completely submerged and you should see small air bubbles escaping the jars. If the jars are floating, your lid is on too tight.
7. Let cook for 30 minutes. Remove from water bath and place on a towel. Let cool slightly before serving, or transfer to fridge once completely cooled.

EGGS & LOX

When you're craving a bagel but your body needs protein, this breakfast has your back. All the essentials of bagels and lox, in egg bite form! Bonus points if you top these bites with red onion.

6 Servings

Ingredients
Cooking spray
8 eggs
1 cup heavy cream
4 oz cream cheese
2 tsp salt
½ tsp ground black pepper
1 tsp Italian seasoning (or your favorite unsalted dried herb blend)
1/3 cup smoked salmon, torn into pieces
2 tbsp capers
Sliced red onion, for garnish (optional)

Directions
1. Get immersion circulator setup and start preheating water bath to 185 degrees F. This is a hot temperature for sous vide cooking: don't forget to place a trivet under your container!
2. Prepare 6 half pint sized jars, all should have undamaged lids. Remove lids and thoroughly spray interior with cooking spray.
3. Crack the eggs into the blender and add the heavy cream and cream cheese. Add the salt, pepper, and Italian seasoning to your blender and blend until completely combined, no individual white or yellow chunks.
4. Pour the egg mixture into prepared jars, dividing evenly between the jars.
5. Evenly distribute the smoked salmon and capers between the jars. Give each jar a small stir to just incorporate the ingredients.
6. Place the undamaged lids on your jars. Close to "finger tight" (you should be able to easily unscrew with just your fingertips).
7. Drop jars carefully into water. Jars should be completely submerged and you should see small air bubbles escaping the jars. If the jars are floating, your lid is on too tight.
8. Let cook for 30 minutes. Remove from water bath and place on a towel. Let cool slightly before serving, or transfer to fridge once completely cooled.
9. Garnish with red onion upon serving if desired.

Overnight Oats

I know what you're thinking: I can already make overnight oats. Without sous vide. And I hear you. But do you really like cold oatmeal? Because I definitely do not. If you're with me, you can do almost the exact prep you normally would for overnight oats, but drop your jar into a water bath instead of into the fridge before bed. Then literally wake up to breakfast made. Morning self will be very pleased with your productive evening self.

This is not a section where you get to play with time and temp. It's going to cook for a long time at 155 degrees F. The time is relatively flexible: anytime between 8 and 10 hours.

The method is simple: 1/3 cup steel oats + 1 1/3 cup liquid, with some goodies stirred in. Feel free to play with the toppings and the liquid you use for cooking, but I've shared my favorites here.

To reheat, remove the lid and pop these boys in the microwave for 2 - 3 minutes, stirring every 30 seconds.

Blueberry Ginger OVERNIGHT OATS

This overnight oats recipe is veering on super food. Blueberries bring the antioxidants and fiber, while ginger comes in with anti-inflammatory goodness. Not to mention, the steel oats are going to keep you full all the livelong day.

1 Serving

Ingredients
1/3 cup steel cut oats
1 1/3 cups milk
1 tbsp honey
1 tsp grated ginger
¼ cup blueberries

Directions
1. Get immersion circulator setup and start preheating water bath to 155 degrees F. Make sure there is a trivet underneath the water bath.
2. Add all ingredients to a pint-sized jar.
3. Place the undamaged lid on your jar. Close to "finger tight" (you should be able to easily unscrew with just your fingertips). Shake to combine. Drop jar carefully into water. Jar should be completely submerged and you should see small air bubbles escaping. If the jar is floating, your lid is on too tight.
4. Let cook for 8-10 hours. Remove from water bath and place on a towel. Let cool slightly before serving, or transfer to fridge once completely cooled.

Banana Almond Butter
OVERNIGHT OATS

This is not an exciting flavor combination, but it's a delicious staple. You can use whatever nut butter you'd like, but almond butter + banana makes my heart sing, and I just know you'll feel the same.

1 Serving

Ingredients
1/3 cup steel cut oats
1 1/3 cups milk
1 tbsp honey
1 tbsp almond butter
½ banana, thinly sliced

Directions
1. Get your immersion circulator setup and start preheating water bath to 155 degrees F. Make sure there is a trivet underneath the water bath.
2. Add all ingredients except bananas to a pint-sized jar.
3. Place the undamaged lid on your jar. Close to "finger tight" (you should be able to easily unscrew with just your fingertips). Shake to combine all ingredients. Drop jar carefully into water. Jar should be completely submerged and you should see small air bubbles escaping. If the jar is floating, your lid is on too tight.
4. Let cook for 8-10 hours. Remove from water bath and place on a towel. Let cool slightly before serving, or transfer to fridge once completely cooled. Top with banana slices.

Maple Pecan OVERNIGHT OATS

Oatmeal is good, but do you know what makes it even better? Something that interrupts the texture. Enter pecans! And their BFF, maple syrup. All the flavors of an extravagant brunch, ready for you when you wake up in the morning.

1 Serving

Ingredients
1/3 cup steel cut oats
1 1/3 cups milk
¼ tsp salt
½ tsp cinnamon
2 tbsp maple syrup
1 tbsp chopped roasted pecans

Directions
1. Get immersion circulator setup and start preheating water bath to 155 degrees F. Make sure there is a trivet underneath the water bath.
2. Add all ingredients to a pint-sized jar.
3. Place the undamaged lid on your jar. Close to "finger tight" (you should be able to easily unscrew with just your fingertips). Shake to combine all ingredients. Drop jar carefully into water. Jar should be completely submerged and you should see small air bubbles escaping. If the jar is floating, your lid is on too tight.
4. Let cook for 8-10 hours. Remove from water bath and place on a towel. Let cool slightly before serving, or transfer to fridge once completely cooled.

Coconut Chai OVERNIGHT OATS

Is there anything so comforting on a cold day as a chai latte? For me, the answer is no: it's like coziness in a cup. These overnight oats are a chai latte in breakfast form, and they make me feel all warm and fuzzy inside.

1 Serving

Ingredients
1/3 cup steel cut oats
1 1/3 cups coconut milk
2 tsp garam masala
1 tbsp honey
Optional garnish: toasted coconut

Directions
1. Get immersion circulator setup and start preheating water bath to 155 degrees F.
2. Add all ingredients to a pint-sized jar.
3. Place the undamaged lid on your jar. Close to "finger tight" (you should be able to easily unscrew with just your fingertips). Shake to combine. Drop jar carefully into water. Jar should be completely submerged and you should see small air bubbles escaping. If the jar is floating, your lid is on too tight.
4. Let cook for 8-10 hours. Remove from water bath and place on a towel. Let cool slightly before serving, or transfer to fridge once completely cooled.

Pickles

Tiny vegetable
Brine, time, mason jar cocoon
Pickle butterfly
- Eric Cole (Husband)

Pickles are transformative. They say, "Hey, boring food - can I get in on that?" then flip the whole dish on its head. On a sandwich, as part of a cheeseboard, tuna salad, or in one of our nightly "bowls" (your call to check out my Instagram, @aducksoven), they consistently bring the flavor level up to ten. And the pickle recipes in this book? Well, they really do that. Like, really.

Each of these recipes has a "tang" source in addition to your standard vinegar, like ginger, mustard, lemon and pomegranate. They're seriously bold and going to light up your life.

I love sous vide for pickling. Wanna know why? They cook for TWO HOURS. Yes, then they need to sit in the fridge for twelve, but that's a lot shorter than your standard pickling process, which is days at a minimum.

So, are these babies shelf stable? Here's the deal: if you want to take the time to sterilize your jars, they certainly are. If you don't, pop 'em in the fridge. Dealer's choice. I tend to be lazy. Therefore my fridge is packed with pickles.

Curry Spiced PICKLED CARROTS

Where my curry lovers at?! Curry is a polarizing spice blend, but it lights me up. Fragrant coriander, pungent cumin, and spicy peppercorns, it keeps my taste buds on their toes. Carrots are the perfect foil for these big flavors with their mild sweetness. I recommend just snacking on these guys as is, but get creative!

Ingredients
1 pound carrots, peeled and cut into ½ inch wide matchsticks short enough to fit in your jars
½ tsp coriander seeds
½ tsp cumin seeds
½ tsp mustard seeds
½ tsp black peppercorns
1 cinnamon stick, cut into quarters
2 cayenne peppers, seeded and ribs removed, sliced
Thumb-sized piece fresh turmeric, sliced
Thumb-sized piece fresh ginger, sliced
2 cups apple cider vinegar
1½ cups warm water
3 tbsp kosher salt
1 tbsp sugar

Directions
1. Get immersion circulator setup and start preheating water bath to 145 degrees F.
2. Arrange the carrots in pint-sized jars. Do not pack tightly: carrots should be able to move around freely. You'll likely fill 2-4 jars.
3. Evenly divide coriander, cumin, mustard, peppercorns, cinnamon, cayenne, turmeric, and ginger between your jars.
4. Whisk together vinegar, water, salt, and sugar until dissolved. Pour over carrots in jars so they're completely covered. Top with equal parts water and vinegar if you need more liquid.
5. Use undamaged lids to close jars. Close to "finger tight" (you should be able to easily unscrew with your fingertips). Drop jars carefully into water. Jars should be completely submerged.
6. Cook for 2 hours. Remove from water and let cool for 12 hours. See page 33 for storage instructions.

Lemon
PICKLED ASPARAGUS

This was the first pickle recipe I ever wrote, and HOLY WOW, few times have I ever had such a clear winner in my first round of recipe development. My parents picked Husband and I up to run errands right after I'd made them, so I grabbed a jar to bring in the car and they were gone by the time we got to our destination. They might change your life.

Ingredients
1 bunch of asparagus, woody ends removed
1 peeled and crushed clove of garlic per jar
2 pieces of lemon rind per jar
3 sprigs of dill per jar
2 cups apple cider vinegar
1½ cups warm water
¼ cup lemon juice
3 tbsp kosher salt
1 tbsp sugar

Directions
1. Get immersion circulator setup and start preheating water bath to 145 degrees F.
2. Add stalks of asparagus, garlic, lemon rind, and dill to 2-3 pint-sized jars. Do not pack tightly: asparagus should be able to move around freely.
3. Whisk together vinegar, water, lemon juice, salt, and sugar until dissolved. Pour over asparagus in jars so they're completely covered. Top with equal parts water and vinegar if you need more liquid.
4. Use undamaged lids to close jars. Close to "finger tight" (you should be able to easily unscrew with your fingertips). Drop jars carefully into water. Jars should be completely submerged.
5. Cook for 2 hours. Remove from water and let cool for 12 hours. See page 33 for storage instructions.

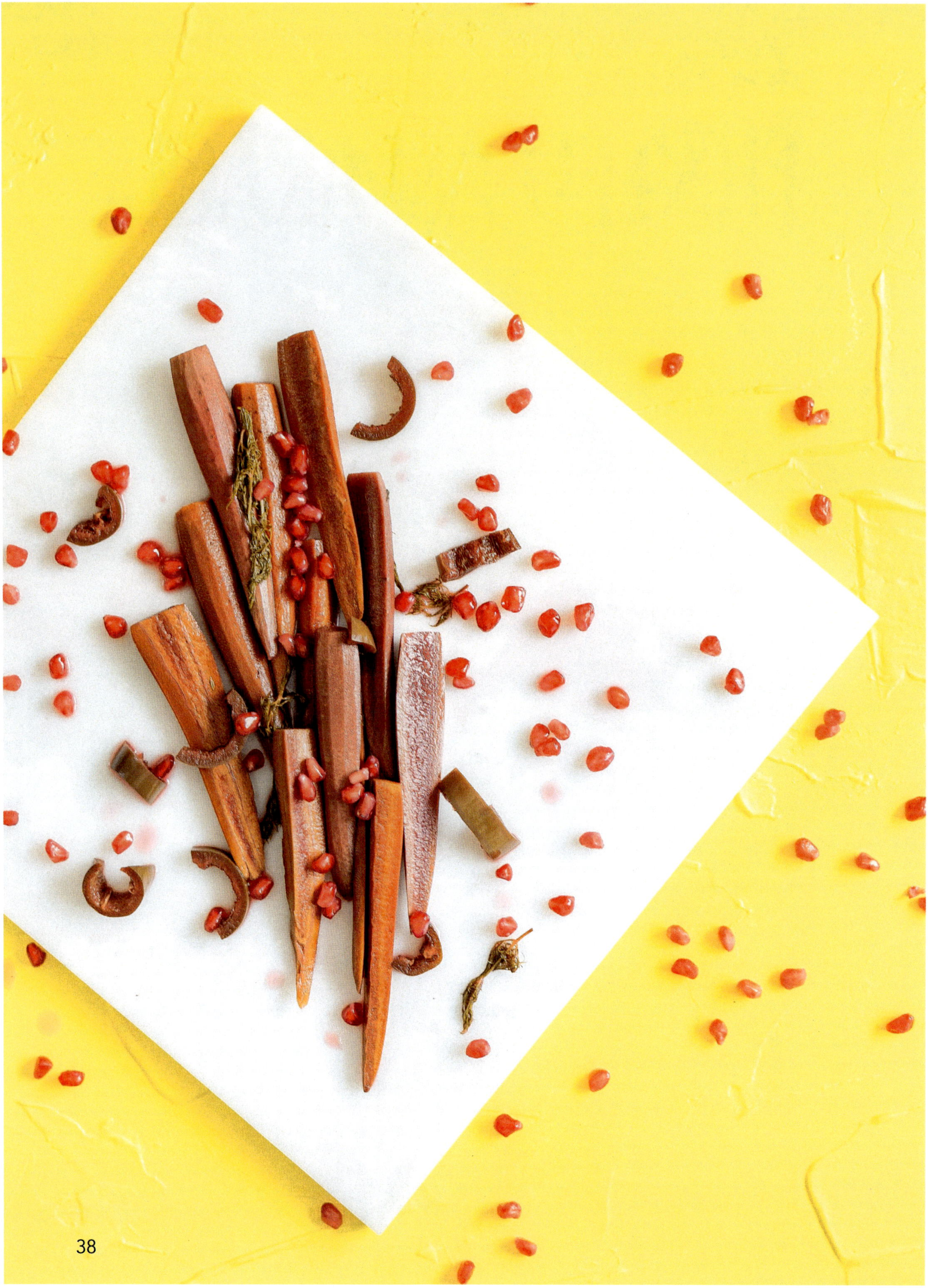

Spicy Pomegranate PICKLED CARROTS

This is the type of pickle you add to a cheeseboard when you want to impress your friends. It's sweet, it's tangy, it's spicy, and man alive does it pair well with hard, salty cheeses. It's not for the faint of heart. It's big, it's bold, and it's unapologetic.

Ingredients
1 pound carrots, peeled and cut into ½ inch wide matchsticks short enough to fit in your jars
2 jalapenos, ribs and seeds removed, sliced
6 sprigs of dill
6 cloves of garlic
2 cups apple cider vinegar
1 cup warm water
1 cup pomegranate juice, warmed
3 tbsp kosher salt
1 tbsp sugar

Directions
1. Get immersion circulator setup and start preheating water bath to 145 degrees F.
2. Arrange the carrots in pint-sized jars. Do not pack tightly: carrots should be able to move around freely. You'll likely fill 2-4 jars.
3. Evenly divide jalapenos, dill, and garlic between your jars.
4. Whisk together vinegar, water, pomegranate juice, salt, and sugar until dissolved. Pour over carrots in jars so they're completely submered. Top with equal parts water and vinegar if you need more liquid.
5. Use undamaged lids to close jars. Close to "finger tight" (you should be able to easily unscrew with your fingertips).
6. Drop jars carefully into water. Jars should be completely submerged.
7. Cook for 2 hours. Remove from water and let cool for 12 hours. See page 33 for storage instructions.

Pro tip: Have a Trader Joe's near you? They carry pomegranate vinegar. If you can get it, do 2 cups of pomegranate vinegar and 2 cups of warm water instead of the 1 cup water, 1 cup juice, and 2 cups apple cider vinegar.

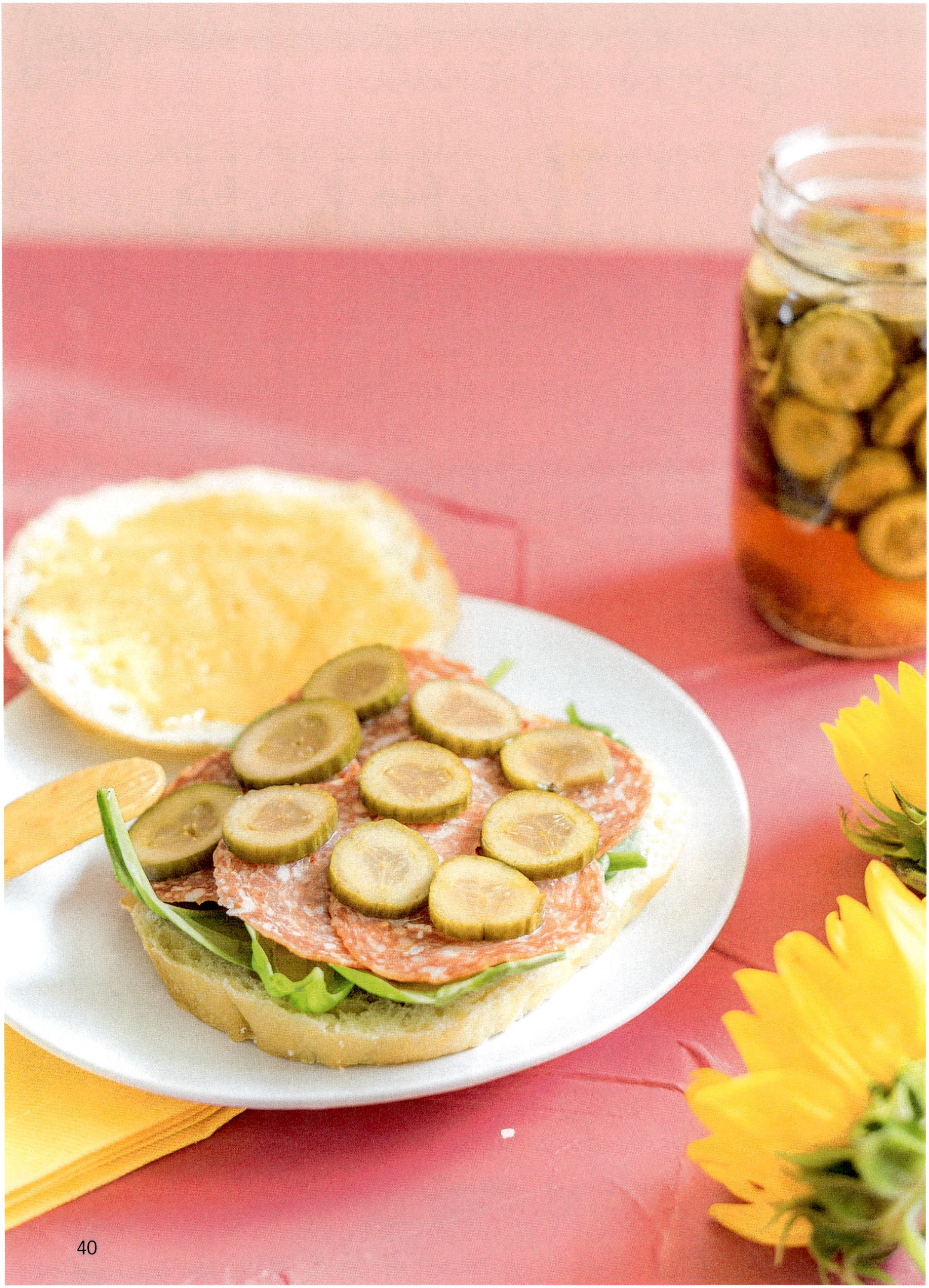

Smoky Mustard SANDWICH PICKLES

These are like your standard cucumber pickle, but the smoky component adds a whole new dimension. It's the perfect sandwich pickle. The hint of smoke changes the entire flavor profile of something like a Cubano and makes a standard cheeseburger interesting. Put them on a pulled pork sandwich, I dare you.

Ingredients
2 cucumbers, sliced into ¼ inch slices (or your desired pickle thickness!)
6 cloves of garlic
6 springs of dill
1 tbsp mustard seeds
2 cups white vinegar
2 tbsp liquid smoke
1½ cups warm water
3 tbsp kosher salt
1 tbsp sugar

Directions
1. Get immersion circulator setup and start preheating water bath to 145 degrees F.
2. Add cucumbers, garlic, dill, and mustard seeds to pint-sized jars. Do not pack tightly: veggies should be able to move around freely.
3. Whisk together vinegar, water, liquid smoke, salt, and sugar until dissolved. Pour over veggies in jars.
4. Use undamaged lids to close jars. Close to "finger tight" (you should be able to easily unscrew with your fingertips). Drop jars carefully into water. Jars should be completely submerged.
5. Cook for 2 hours. Remove from water and let cool for 12 hours. See page 33 for storage instructions.

42

Pork Chops

Pork chops: the world's most boring dinner. The fear of children everywhere. The cut of meat you inevitably overcook. No more. Get ready for succulent, savory cuts of meat that are full of flavor. Like can't put your fork and knife down type of good.

The sous vide transforms this usually dry, boring cut of meat because you can avoid overcooking it while still tenderizing it and rendering down the beautiful, flavorful fat. Real talk: while my photography assistant (hi, mom!) and I were shooting photos for this section of the book, we couldn't stop eating the subject. Oh, the perks of food photography.

A few of these recipes incorporate a fun technique: your sauce cooks in its own bag in the bath right alongside the pork. This girl loves efficiency.

I've done a lot of experimenting with temperatures for the pork chops and found my personal preference: 145 degrees F. It still has the temperature I expect of a pork chop and is more of a medium. If you like your pork a little rarer and a little less toothy, I recommend trying 140 degrees F.

I like to cook my pork chops for 1-2 hours, but you can go longer if you like. I wouldn't recommend going longer than 4, as the texture will start to get affected (and not in a good way).

Rare *(a little squeaky)* — 130 degrees F
Medium-Rare *(juicy, meaty, tender)* — 140 degrees F
Medium *(firm, meaty, but still juicy)* — 145 degrees F
Medium-Well *(firm, starting to dry)* — 150 degrees F

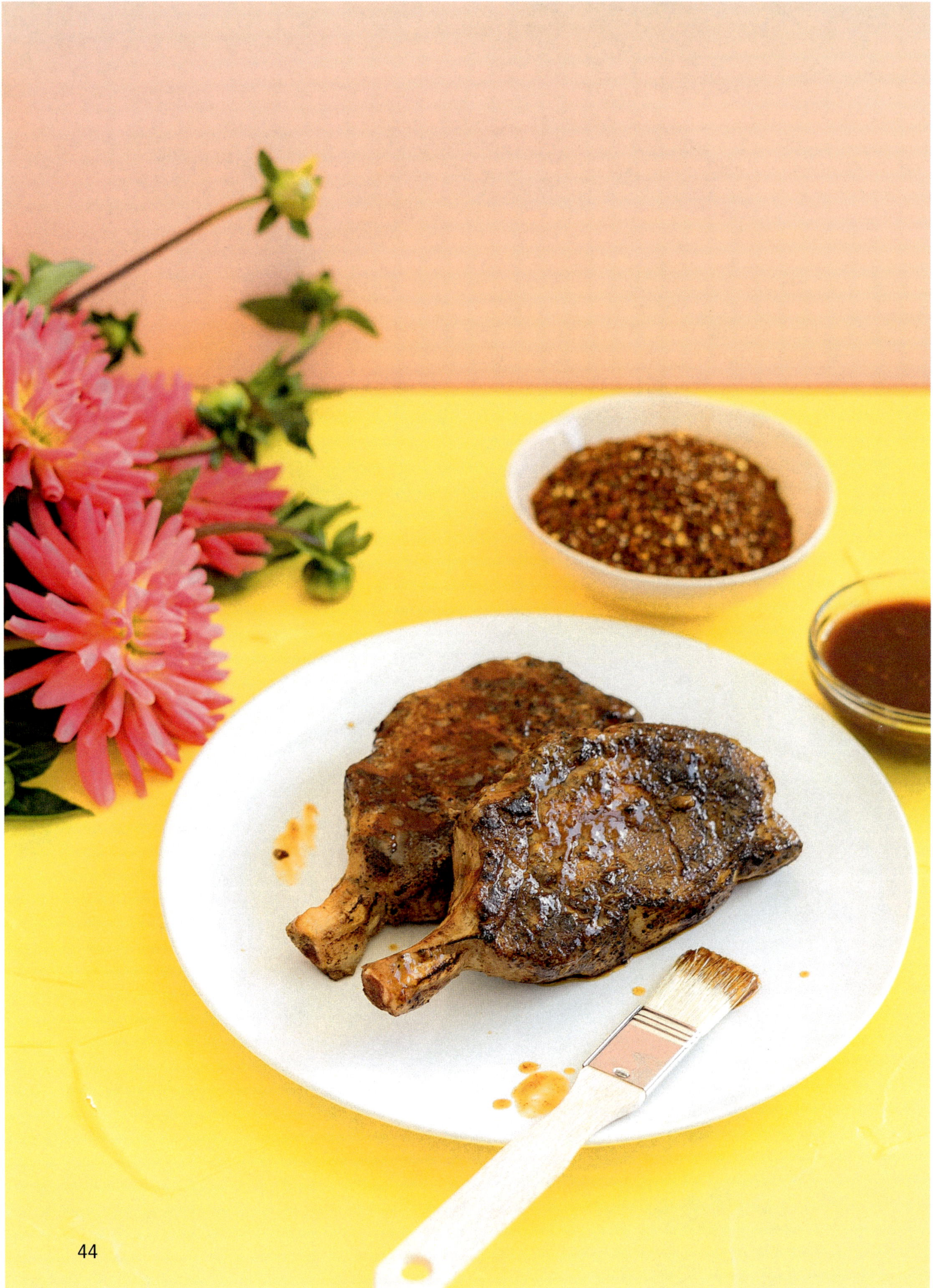

Coffee and Chili Rubbed PORK CHOPS

I know what you're thinking: coffee and chili? Hang with me here. Coffee adds a whole new depth to this somewhat traditional rub and intensifies the chili flavor. This dish smells and tastes so good, you'll be lucky if it makes it to the dinner table before you've finished sneaking bites "here and there."

2 Servings

Ingredients
2 large pork chops
2 tbsp finely ground dark-roast coffee
2 tbsp chili powder
2 tbsp dark brown sugar, tightly packed
1 tbsp smoked paprika
1 tbsp kosher salt
1 tsp ground cumin
1 tsp red pepper flakes
1 tbsp ghee
Your favorite BBQ sauce (optional)

Directions
1. Get immersion circulator setup and start preheating water bath to 145 degrees F (or temp of your choice from page 43).
2. In a bowl, combine all ingredients except pork chops and ghee.
3. Rub pork with seasoning mixture until thoroughly coated.
4. Add pork chops to your bag of choice for sous vide cooking (page 9), remove the air, and seal.
5. Add bag to water and let cook for 1 - 2 hours.
6. When pork chops are done, heat a cast iron skillet on high heat. Add the ghee and melt.
7. Remove the pork chops from water bath and bag. Sear in cast iron skillet on each side until just browned.
8. Serve with your favorite BBQ sauce if desired.

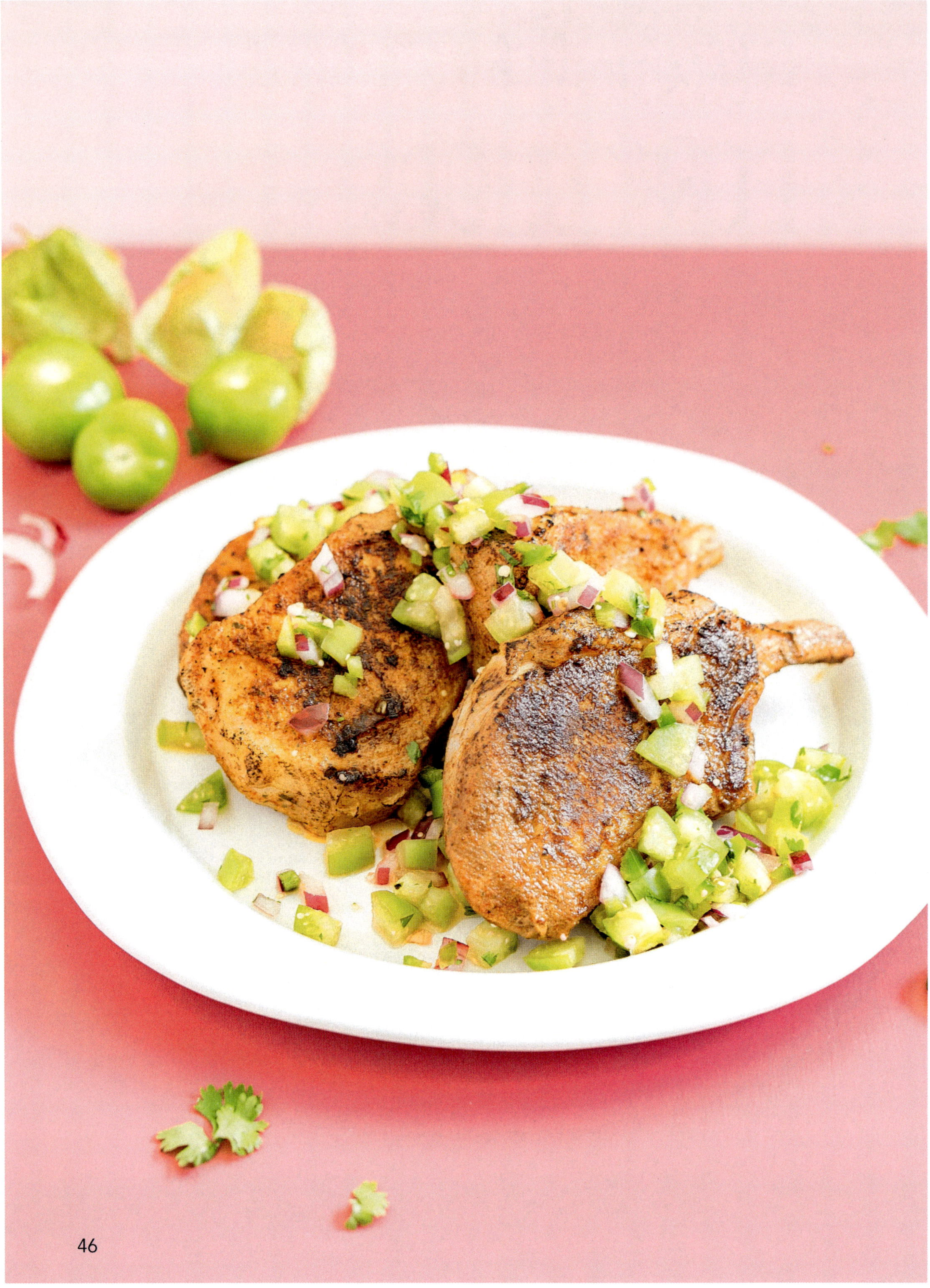

Salsa Verde PORK CHOPS

This dish is a show-stopper, a show-show-stopper in both taste and appearance. The pork chops get seasoned with a smoky, savory spice blend then hit with a bright sauce in the form of salsa verde that cooks right alongside the pork chops.

2 Servings

Ingredients
2 large pork chops
2 tsp kosher salt
¼ tsp black pepper
2 tsp chili powder
1 tsp garlic powder
1 tsp onion powder
6 tomatillos, diced
1 jalapeno, minced
2 limes
¼ red onion, finely chopped
¼ cup cilantro, chopped
1 tbsp ghee

Directions
1. Get immersion circulator setup and start preheating water bath to 145 degrees F (or temp of your choice from page 43).
2. Mix together the salt, pepper, chili powder, garlic powder, and onion powder in a small bowl. Season pork chops with the spice mixture. Add pork chops to your bag of choice for sous vide cooking (page 9), remove the air, and seal.
3. Add bag to water and let cook for 1 - 2 hours.
4. Once you've dropped the pork chops, start on the salsa verde. In your bag of choice, add the tomatillos, jalapeno, limes, onion, and cilantro. Remove the air, seal, and drop into the water with the pork chops. Cook until pork chops are done.
5. When pork chops are done, heat a cast iron skillet on high heat. Add the ghee and melt.
6. Remove the pork chops from water bath and bag. Sear in cast iron skillet on each side until just browned. Set aside to rest.
7. Remove the salsa verde from the bath. Spoon over the pork chops to serve.

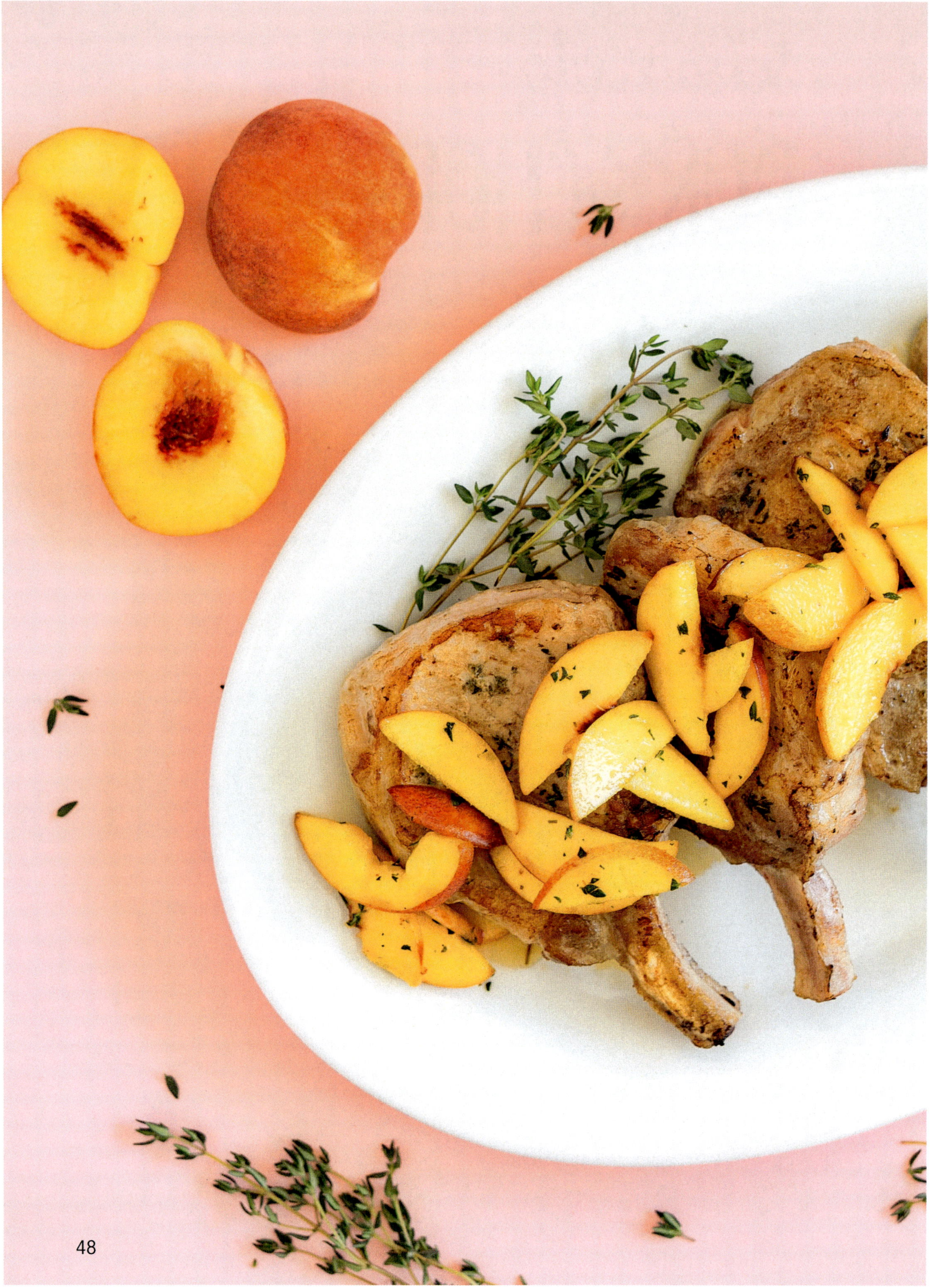

Spicy Peach and Thyme PORK CHOPS

Peaches and pork: we know they go well together. But add a little cayenne and thyme to the mix and oh my gooosh, the game has changed. The peaches break down just enough and are served warm on top of savory, herby pork chops. Need I say more?

2 Servings

Ingredients
2 large pork chops
Salt and pepper
2 tbsp fresh thyme, chopped and divided
3 peaches, pitted and sliced
1 tbsp honey
¼ tsp cayenne pepper
1 tbsp butter
1 tbsp ghee

Directions
1. Get immersion circulator setup and start preheating water bath to 145 degrees F (or temp of your choice from page 43).
2. Season pork chops with salt, pepper, and half the fresh thyme.
3. Add pork chops to your bag of choice for sous vide cooking (page 9), remove the air, and seal.
4. Add bag to water and let cook for 1 - 2 hours.
5. Once you've dropped the pork chops, start on the peaches. In your bag of choice, add peaches, honey, cayenne pepper, and butter. Remove the air, seal, and drop into the water with the pork chops. Cook until pork chops are done.
6. When pork chops are done, heat a cast iron skillet on high heat. Add the ghee and melt.
7. Remove the pork chops from water bath and bag. Sear in cast iron skillet on each side until just browned. Set aside to rest.
8. Remove the peaches from the bath. Spoon over the pork chops to serve.

50

Tomato Balsamic PORK CHOPS

This is the type of dish that you must pair with a really good (okay, at least decent) bottle of red wine. Tangy balsamic and tomatoes are a match made in heaven, especially with pork. My favorite part? It's super easy to throw together. Feel like seriously cheating? Use a can of diced tomatoes. I won't tell.

2 Servings

Ingredients
2 large pork chops
Salt and pepper for seasoning
2 tomatoes, diced
¼ cup balsamic vinegar
½ tsp salt
1 tsp sugar
1 tbsp ghee

Directions
1. Get immersion circulator setup and start preheating water bath to 145 degrees F (or temp of your choice from page 43).
2. Season pork chops with salt and pepper.
3. Add the tomatoes, balsamic vinegar, salt, and sugar to your bag of choice for sous vide cooking (page 9). Give it a good shake to mix together the ingredients. Add the pork chops, move the liquid around to coat, remove the air using the water displacement method (page 10), and seal.
4. Add bag to water and let cook for 1 - 2 hours.
5. When pork chops are done, heat a cast iron skillet on high heat. Add the ghee and melt.
6. Remove the pork chops from water bath and bag. Sear in cast iron skillet on each side until just browned. Set aside to rest.
7. Spoon remaining liquid in bag over the pork chops to serve.

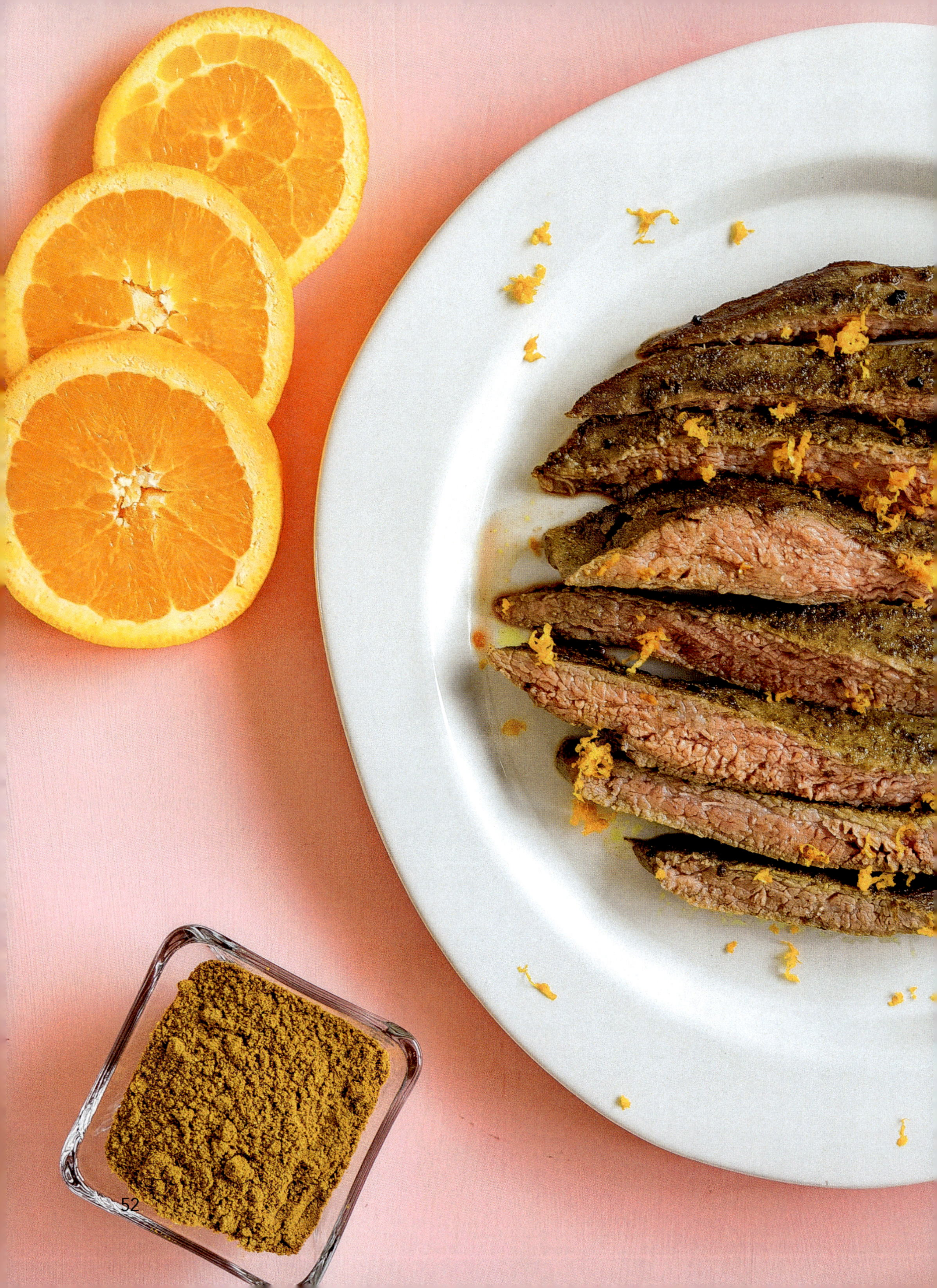

Steak

Steak is the whole reason sous vide ever caught my interest. I grew up in a carnivorous home, to say the least. Drop by my parents' house for dinner on any given night, and you'll see plates full of ribeye steaks, fresh caught salmon, and veggies. I am a lucky girl.

Once I moved out on my own, I found that steak was a really difficult thing to cook correctly. It didn't help that in college I never had a grill and never lived in a place long enough to really get to know a stove and how it cooks. Steaks in my house were perpetually over- or undercooked. And that's a tragedy.

Husband eventually got pretty good at cooking steaks on our grill when we got one, but they were still annoying to babysit and plan your entire meal around. That definitely didn't stop us from cooking and eating them, but man, am I excited to have found a better way.

I can drop steaks in the water bath, prepare the sides, and those steaks are done when I tell them they're done, dammit! I am no longer beholden to a couple of tri-tips.

Okay, time and temp. I'm sure you could have predicted this: I like a steak cooked to medium-rare. Pick a temperature for your liking, but please, for me, do not cook a steak past medium-well. It's just wrong.

As we talked about in the beginning of the book, you shouldn't let your food hang out in the water bath longer than 3 hours if you're cookin' lower than 130 degrees F.

Rare *(pink-red interior, soft)*	123 degrees F
Medium-Rare *(pink, tender)*	129 degrees F
Medium *(pink, starting to firm)*	135 degrees F
Medium-Well *(barely pink)*	143 degrees F

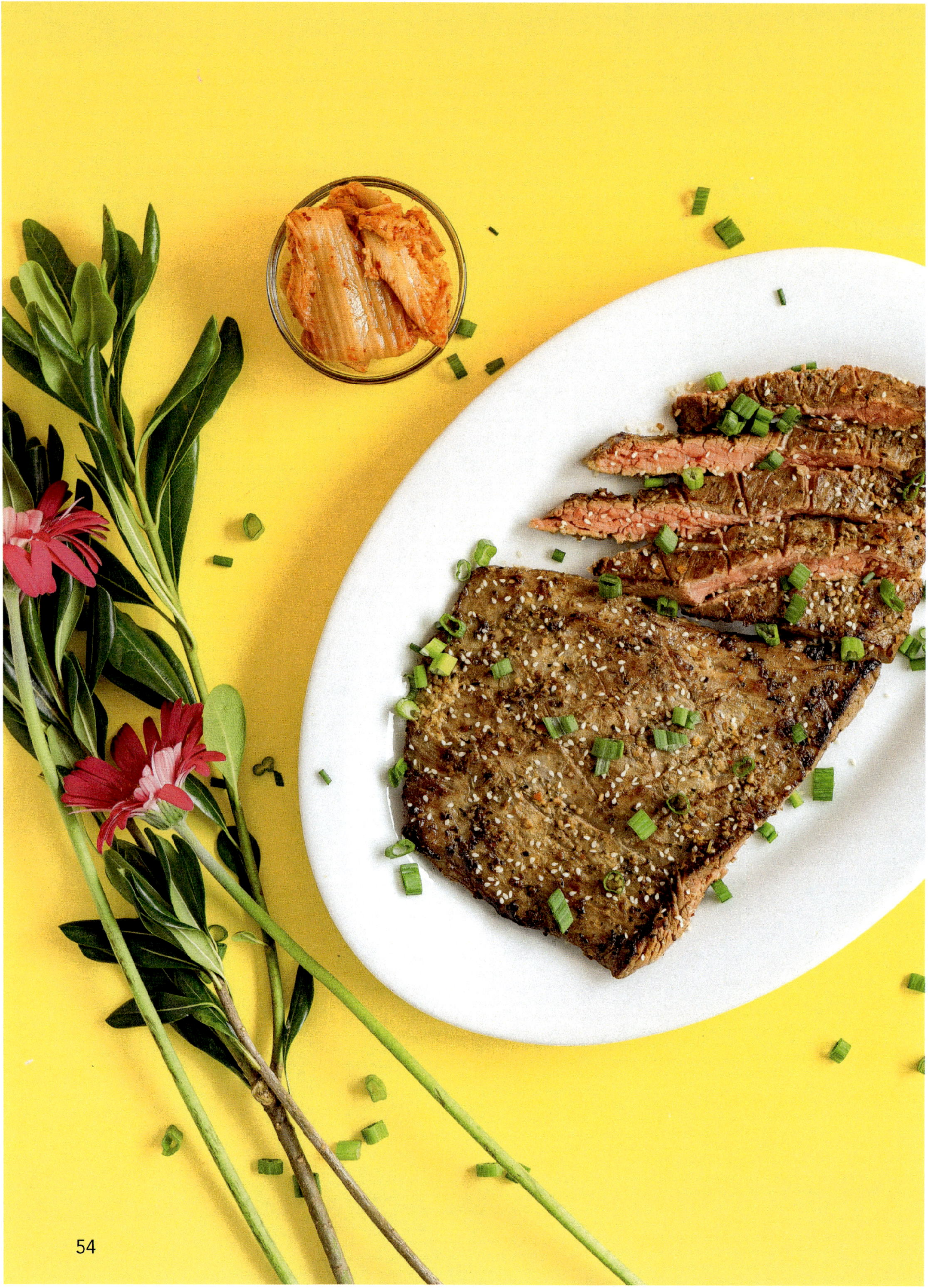

Korean
FLANK STEAK

I love Korean food. Love. It. When my mom helped me move, she offered to unpack my kitchen (she's a generous woman) and was horrified by the number of condiments I have. These condiments include multiple varieties of kimchi, gochujang hot sauce, and even liquid kimchi. All of which pair beautifully with this Korean Flank Steak, called Bulgogi.

6 Servings

Ingredients
1 tbsp gochujang
1 tbsp rice vinegar
1 tbsp soy sauce
2 tsp grated peeled ginger
1 tsp minced garlic
1 ½ tsp sesame oil
1 tsp red pepper flakes
2 pound flank steak
Salt and pepper
1 tbsp ghee

Directions
1. Get immersion circulator setup and start preheating water bath to 129 degrees F (or temp of your choice from page 53).
2. Score the flank steak with a sharp knife in diagonal lines across the steak both directions.
3. Mix together all ingredients except the steak and ghee.
4. Add the steak to your sous vide bag of choice (page 9) and pour gochujang mixture over the steak.
5. Remove the air from the bag using the water displacement method (page 10).
6. Add the bag to the water bath and cook for 2-3 hours.
7. Preheat a cast iron skillet over high heat. Add ghee to skillet and melt.
8. Remove steak from water bath and bag. Thoroughly pat dry with paper towels and season with salt and pepper. Sear on both sides until just browned.
9. Let rest on cutting board for 5 minutes. When done, slice against the grain into 1 inch strips. Serve with white rice and kimchi.

RAS EL HANOUT

Ingredients
1 tsp salt
1 tsp ground cumin
1 tsp ground ginger
1 tsp ground turmeric
3/4 tsp ground cinnamon
3/4 tsp freshly ground black pepper
1/2 tsp ground coriander seed
1/2 tsp ground cayenne pepper
1/2 tsp ground allspice
1/2 tsp ground nutmeg
1/4 tsp ground cloves

Directions
In a small bowl, mix together all ingredients until evenly combined. Store in an airtight container at room temperature.

Moroccan
FLANK STEAK

This recipe is full of fragrant, warm flavors and is truly one of my favorite ways to eat flank steak. It's the kind of steak that makes you go back for seconds, then thirds and it tastes great with any side dish you feel like pairing it with (especially cinnamon ginger sweet potatoes - see page 109). A light red like a pinot noir is my favorite thing to drink with this masterpiece.

6 Servings

Ingredients
2 pound flank steak
Olive oil
1 tbsp ras el hanout spice blend
1 tsp kosher salt
1 tbsp orange zest
1 tbsp ghee
Salt and pepper

Directions
1. Get immersion circulator setup and start preheating water bath to 129 degrees F (or temp of your choice from page 53).
2. Score the flank steak with a sharp knife in diagonal lines across the steak both directions.
3. Rub olive oil into the steak all over both sides. It shouldn't be dripping, but should be well coated.
4. Season both sides of the steak evenly with ras el hanout, kosher salt, and orange zest.
5. Add to bag and remove the air using your method of choice (page 10). Add the bag to the water bath and cook for 2-3 hours.
6. Preheat a cast iron skillet over high heat. Add ghee to skillet to melt.
7. Remove steak from water bath and bag. Thoroughly pat dry with paper towels and season with salt and pepper. Sear on both sides until just browned.
8. Let rest on cutting board for 5 minutes. When done, slice against the grain into 1 inch strips.

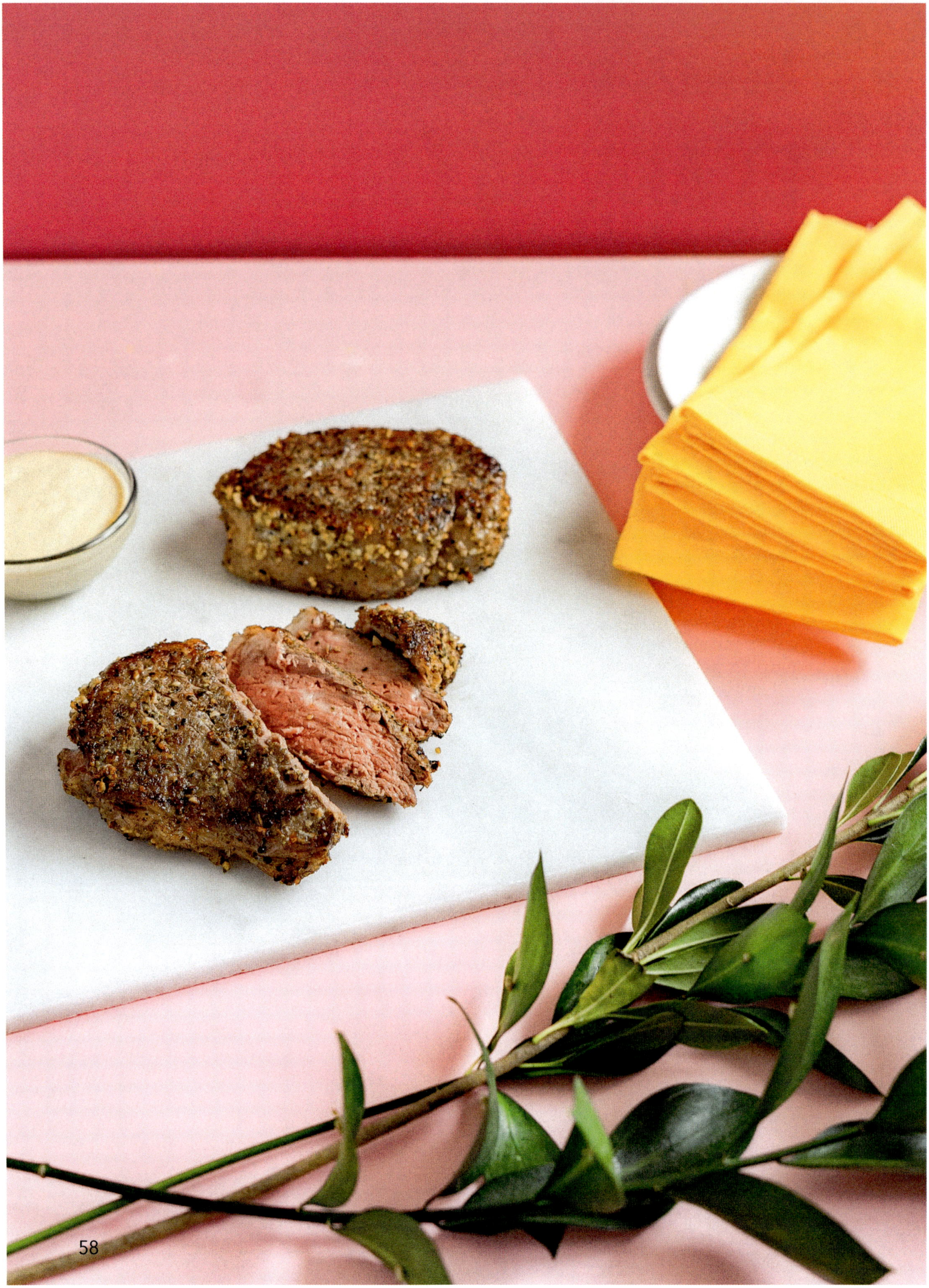

UMAMI RIBEYE

This recipe is for the folks who like big, bold, funky flavors. The marinade has every umami-packed ingredient I could think of, resulting in a steak that just screams at you when you take a bite. The fatty, rich ribeye pairs perfectly with the bright, tangy flavors of the marinade. Pour yourself a big, bold red wine, pair with Garlicky Mashed Potatoes (page 105) and you've got yourself a meal.

2 Servings

Ingredients
4 cloves of garlic
3 anchovy fillets
2 tbsp tomato paste
1 tbsp sundried tomatoes
1 tbsp Worcestershire sauce
1 tbsp soy sauce
1 tbsp olive oil
¼ tsp black pepper
2 8 oz ribeye steaks
1 tbsp ghee
Salt and pepper

Directions
1. Add all ingredients except ghee and steak to a food processor. Blend until completely smooth. If it's too thick, add a little more olive oil and continue blending. It should be a little thinner than a paste.
2. Add steaks and umami mixture to your bag of choice for sous vide cooking (page 9). Remove all the air using the water displacement method (page 10). Place in refrigerator and let marinate for at least 4 hours before cooking.
3. Get immersion circulator setup and start preheating water bath to 129 degrees F (or temp of your choice from page 53).
4. Drop the bag into the water bath and cook for 1.5 - 3 hours.
5. Preheat a cast iron skillet over high heat. Add ghee to skillet.
6. Remove the steak from water bath and bag. Thoroughly pat dry with paper towels and season with salt and pepper. Sear on both sides until just browned. Serve immediately.

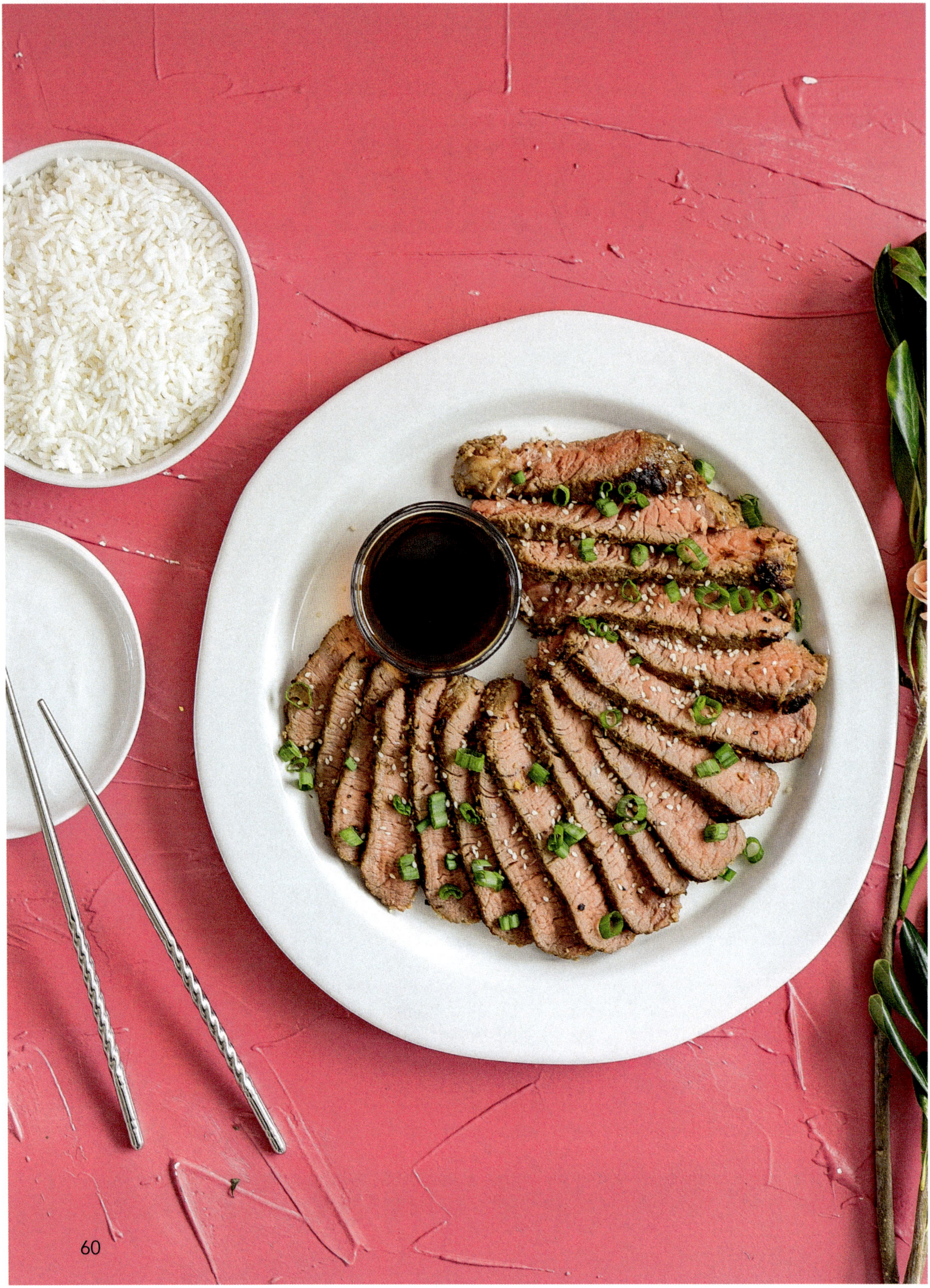

BEEF TATAKI

Now this is a dreamy appetizer. Thinly sliced, very rare beef served with a bright, soy-based dipping sauce. This dish is traditionally served raw and simply seared, but we're cookin' it a little to warm it all the way through and improve the texture a bit. This really is supposed to be served as an appetizer on its own, but I've been known to make a big batch of rice and serve this as a main.

6 Servings

Ingredients
Steak:
1 tbsp sesame oil
1 tsp white sesame seeds
3 tbsp peanut or canola oil
1 tsp red chili flakes
2 pounds center cut, trimmed beef sirloin
Salt and pepper
1 tbsp ghee

Ponzu dipping sauce:
¼ cup soy sauce
¼ cup rice wine vinegar
1 tbsp mirin
2 tbsp lemon juice
2 tbsp grated fresh ginger

6 scallions, sliced thin (for garnish)

Directions
1. Get immersion circulator setup and start preheating water bath to 123 degrees F.
2. Mix together the sesame oil, sesame seeds, oil, and chili flakes.
3. Add the sirloin to your bag of choice. Pour sesame mixture over steaks and rub over the steaks in the bag until completely coated. Remove the air from the bag.
4. Drop the bag into the water bath. Cook for 2 - 3 hours.
5. While the steak is cooking, mix together the ingredients for the ponzu dipping sauce. Set aside.
6. Preheat a cast iron skillet over high heat. Add ghee to skillet.
7. Remove steak from water bath and bag. Thoroughly pat dry with paper towels and season with salt and pepper. Sear on both sides until just browned.
8. When done, slice against the grain into very thin slices (¼ inch at most).
9. Lay on a plate and garnish the steak with the scallions. Dip the meat in the ponzu dipping sauce.

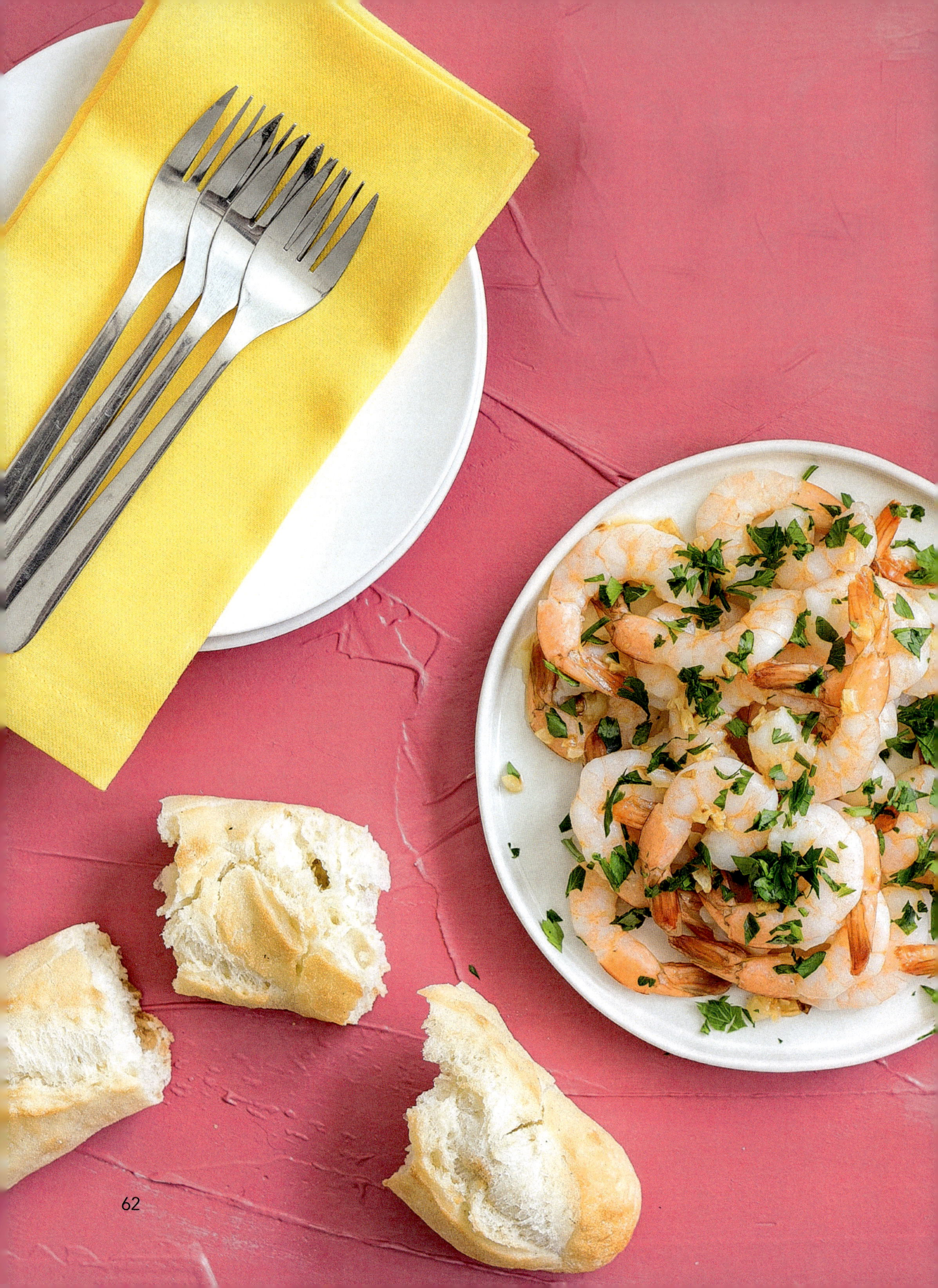

Shrimp

Have you ever eaten overcooked shrimp before? It's seriously gross. They get all small and the texture is so tough. Not. Pleasant. But the idea of undercooking them isn't great either. These little creatures can be annoyingly difficult to cook.

Which is why they're perfect for the sous vide! They reach that temperature sweet spot and don't go any further. In fact, they're one of the easier proteins you'll cook this way since they don't need to be seared: you can go straight from bag to plate.

For many of these recipes, you'll use the water displacement method to get the air out of your bag since there is a lot of liquid in there. See page 10 for instructions on using the water displacement method.

Let's talk time and temp. I like a higher temp that's in the "safety zone" (above 130 degrees F). But you might want to try some of the lower temps. As we talked about in the beginning of the book, you shouldn't let your food hang out in the water bath longer than 3 hours if you're cookin' lower than 130 degrees F. Experiment with temperature all you want, because my recommended cook time is 15 minutes - 1 hour.

Very Rare (almost raw)   125 degrees F
Rare (just starting to firm, tender)   130 degrees F
Medium-Rare (opaque and tender)   135 degrees F
Medium (tender but with a snappy bite)   140 degrees F

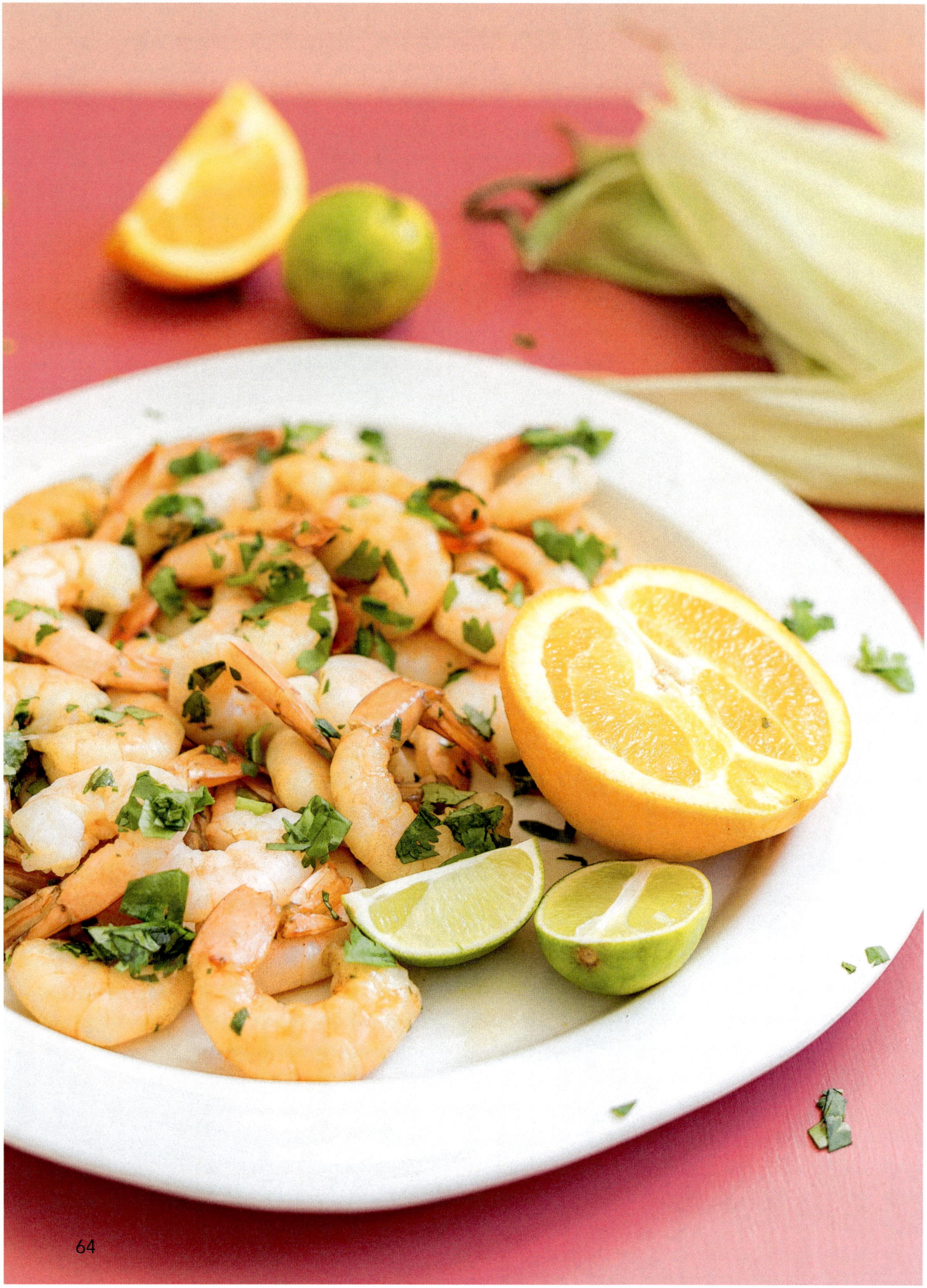

MOJO SHRIMP

Citrus and shrimp are one of my favorite combinations, and this recipe takes things to the next level. We've got orange juice, lime juice, and even some vinegary hot sauce for bright, flavor-packed shrimp. I love this shrimp served simply: rice, maybe a little charred corn, and I'm all set. Pro tip: try this shrimp in tacos some time.

4 Servings

Ingredients
16 oz peeled and deveined shrimp
3 cloves garlic
1/4 cup roughly chopped yellow onion
1/4 cup freshly squeezed orange juice
2 tbsp fresh lime juice
1/4 teaspoon ground cumin
1/4 teaspoon freshly ground black pepper
1/2 teaspoon kosher salt
¼ cup fresh cilantro
1/2 teaspoon hot pepper sauce (e.g. Tabasco™) (optional)
2 tbsp olive oil
1 tbsp fresh chopped cilantro for garnish

Directions
1. Get immersion circulator setup and start preheating water bath to 135 degrees F (or temp of your choice from page 63).
2. Add all ingredients except shrimp and 1 tbsp cilantro to a food processor or blender. Pulse until smooth.
3. Add the shrimp to your bag of choice (page 9). Pour citrus mixture over the shrimp. Remove the air from the bag using the water displacement method (page 10).
4. Drop the bag into the water bath. Cook for 15 minutes - 1 hour.
5. Remove from the bag and serve. Garnish with fresh cilantro.

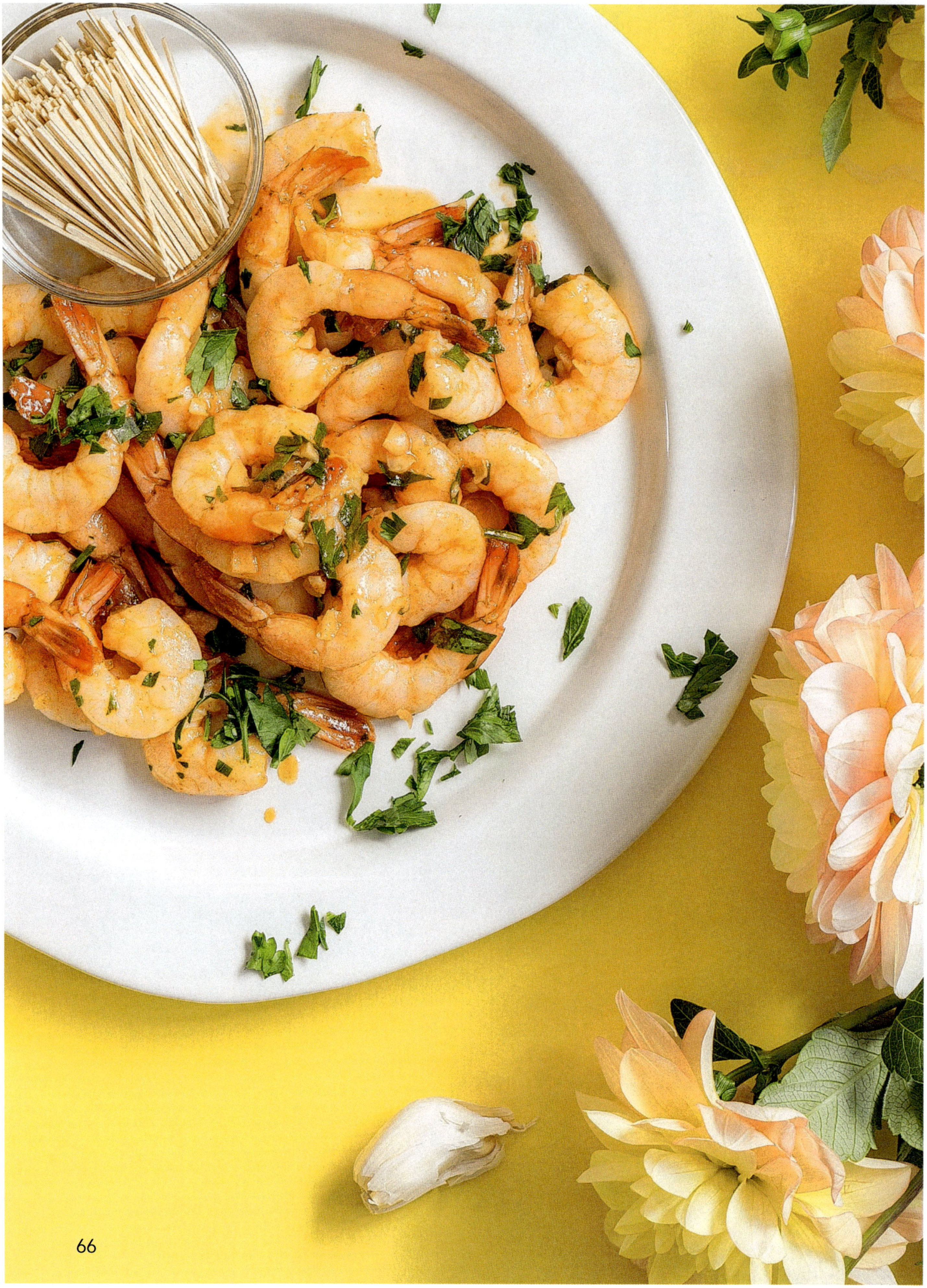

Honey Garlic
SRIRACHA SHRIMP

When I was recipe testing this shrimp, my not-so-little brother came over. I had made over a pound of shrimp, and he ate the entire platter. By himself. In about 7 minutes. Wordlessly. Combine sweet, salty, and spicy, and you've got a winner! This dish makes a great appetizer or main course.

4 Servings

Ingredients
16 oz peeled and deveined shrimp
Salt and pepper
1 tbsp butter, salted
3 cloves garlic, minced
1 tbsp honey
2 tbsp sriracha
1 tbsp chopped parsley, for garnish

Directions
1. Get immersion circulator setup and start preheating water bath to 135 degrees F (or temp of your choice from page 63).
2. Season shrimp with salt and pepper. Set aside.
3. Add butter to a saucepan over medium heat to melt. Once melted, add the garlic. Cook until fragrant.
4. Remove pan from heat. Add the honey and sriracha and stir until completely combined.
5. Add the shrimp to your bag of choice (page 9). Pour sriracha mixture over the shrimp and toss to coat. Remove the air from the bag using the water displacement method (page 10).
6. Drop the bag into the water bath. Cook for 15 minutes - 1 hour.
7. Remove from the bag and serve. Garnish with fresh parsley.

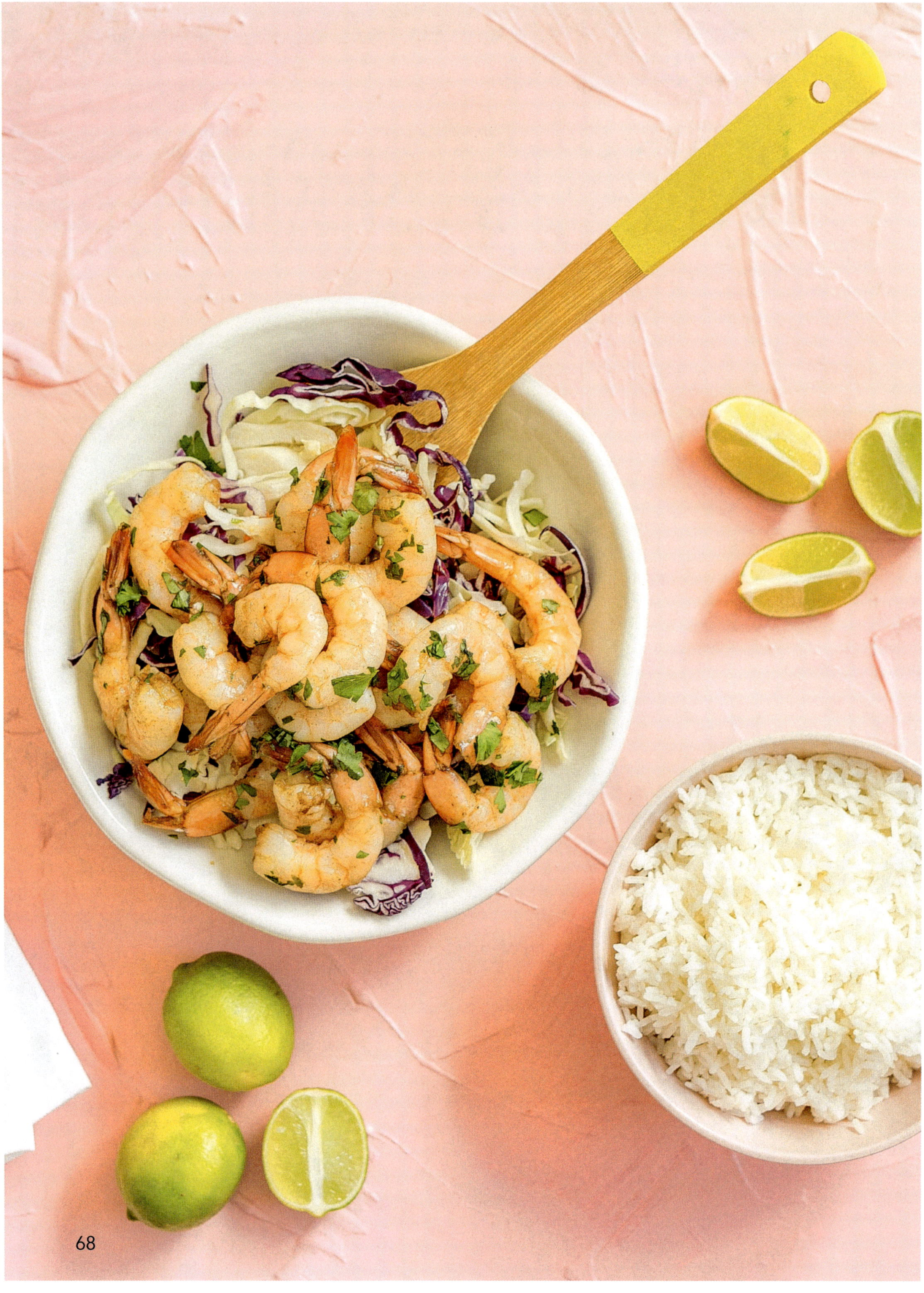

JERK SHRIMP

Usually, we associate jerk seasoning with pork or chicken, but have you ever had it on shrimp? Oh em gee, it is good! Fragrant and just a little spicy, this is simply delicious with just rice and an extra squeeze of lime. If you're looking to sneak in some veggies on this plate, I like to reserve a little of the jerk liquid (before cooking), toss whatever veggies I have on hand in it, and roast them.

4 Servings

Ingredients
16 oz peeled and deveined shrimp
Salt and pepper
3 cloves of garlic, peeled
1/2 onion, chopped
1 jalapeno pepper, seeded and minced
1/3 cup soy sauce
2 tbsp lime juice
1/4 cup olive oil
1 tbsp brown sugar
1 tbsp chopped fresh thyme
1/2 tsp ground cloves
1/2 tsp ground nutmeg
1/2 tsp ground allspice

Directions
1. Get immersion circulator setup and start preheating water bath to 135 degrees F (or temp of your choice from page 63).
2. Season the shrimp with salt and pepper. Set aside. Add remaining ingredients to a food processor or blender. Pulse until smooth.
3. Add the shrimp to your bag of choice (page 9). Pour spice mixture over the shrimp. Remove the air from the bag using the water displacement method (page 10).
4. Drop the bag into the water bath. Cook for 15 minutes - 1 hour.
5. Remove from the bag and serve over steamed white rice.

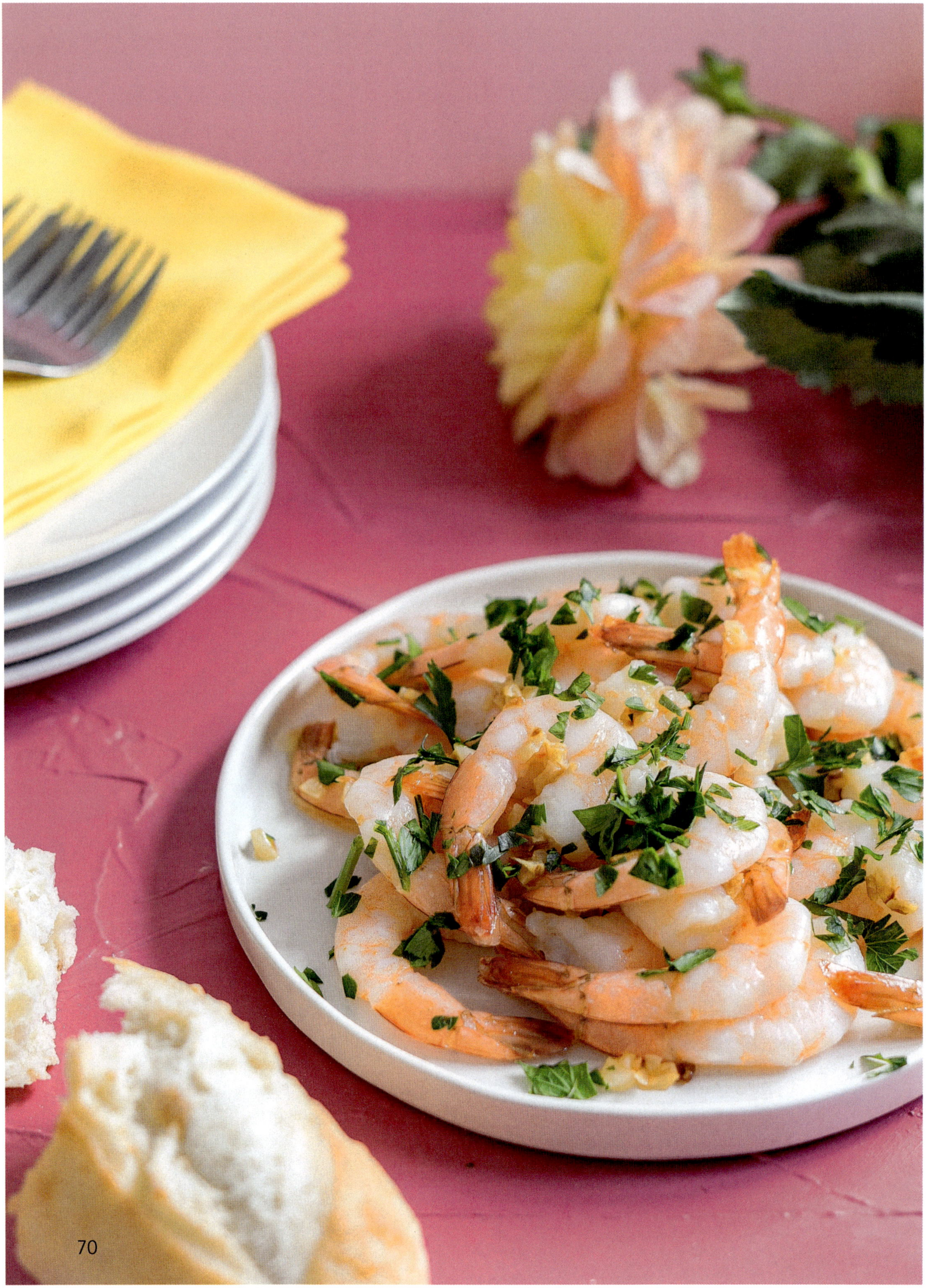

Garlic Butter POACHED SHRIMP

Seafood with a garlic butter sauce: the classic preparation. And for good reason, especially with super low fat shrimp. It makes me think of my childhood, when I would go crabbing with my dad. We'd come home where my mom had plenty of garlic butter and french bread waiting. It was a seafood, butter and bread free for all. These moments are even better as an adult, because I get white wine, too.

4 Servings

Ingredients
16 oz peeled and deveined shrimp
Salt and pepper
3 tbsp butter
5 cloves of garlic, minced
¼ cup dry white wine
¼ cup fresh chopped parsley, 1 tbsp reserved for garnish

Directions
1. Get immersion circulator setup and start preheating water bath to 135 degrees F (or temp of your choice from page 63).
2. Season shrimp with salt and pepper. Set aside.
3. Add butter to a saucepan over medium heat to melt. Once melted, add the garlic. Cook until fragrant, about 3 minutes.
4. Pour white wine into the saucepan. Continue to cook, stirring occasionally, for about 4 minutes.
5. Remove pan from heat. Add the parsley (except the reserved tbsp) and stir until completely combined.
6. Add the shrimp to your bag of choice (page 9). Pour butter mixture over the shrimp and toss to coat. Remove the air from the bag using the water displacement method (page 10).
7. Drop the bag into the water bath. Cook for 15 minutes - 1 hour.
8. Remove from the bag and serve. Garnish with reserved parsley.

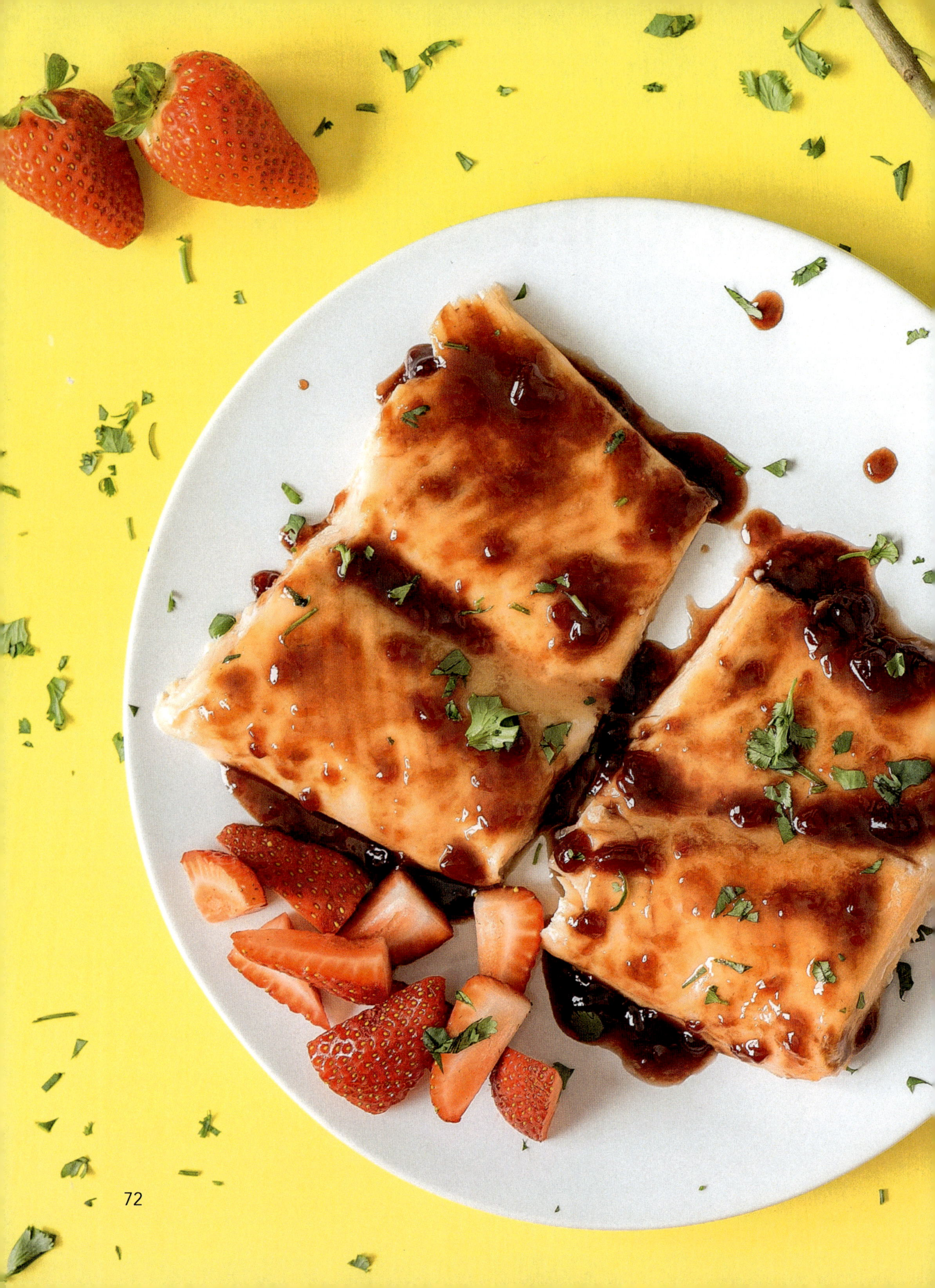

Salmon

Some things you should know about me: my dad is essentially a full-time fisherman and hunter, and I've spent many a summer on his boat. I also worked for a Portland-based sustainable seafood company for a few years. So let's just say seafood is kinda my thing. Salmon, especially. When I was growing up, salmon made a very regular appearance on the dinner table. So much so, in fact, that I got sick of it sometimes. I know, I know: young me sucked.

I love using sous vide for salmon because I love my salmon rare. I mean just kissed by heat. Barely touched. There is nothing sadder than overcooked crumbly salmon, especially when that salmon is a Spring Chinook caught by your dad that morning. The good news? You ain't gonna overcook it when you cook it this way. Man, this gadget is great.

You may not be like me and want your salmon to be cooked so it's a little more than lukewarm. That's fine, I guess. You do you. I'll look away for a moment.

As we talked about in the beginning of the book, you shouldn't let your food hang out in the water bath longer than 3 hours if you're cookin' lower than 130 degrees F. For salmon, we're looking at 45 minutes to an hour. Got it? Good.

Rare *(just barely flaky)*	115 degrees F
Medium-Rare *(moist and fully flaky)*	120 degrees F
Medium-Well *(starting to firm)*	125 degrees F
Well *(completely firm, but still moist)*	130 degrees F

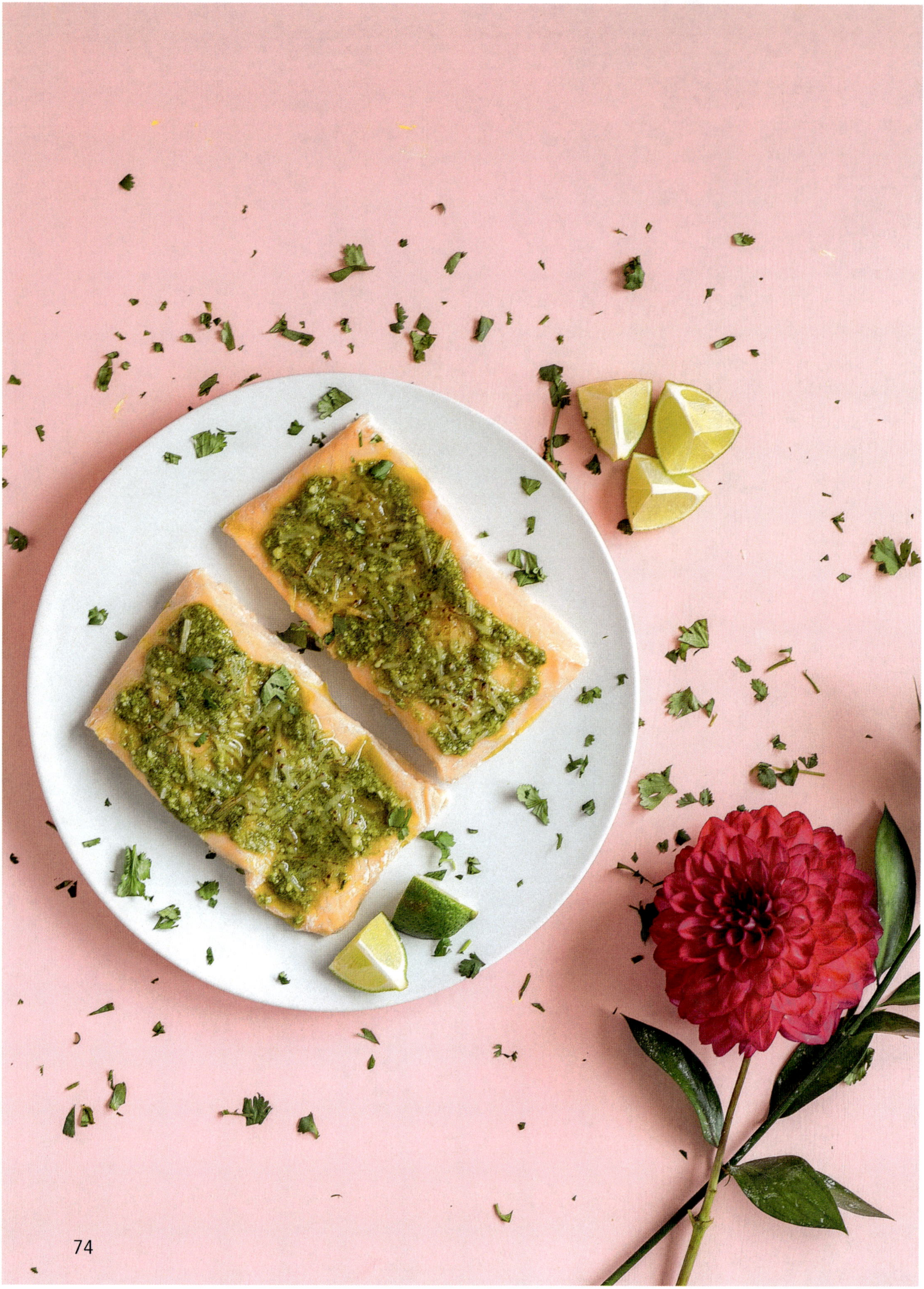

Cilantro Lime Pesto
SALMON

Pesto on salmon: a classic and for good reason. Bright, herby flavors pair so well with this rich, flaky fish. But I'm changin' it up a little. Salmon is a friend of all citrus, not just your usual lemon. Same goes for herbs. You're going to love this variation, pinky swear.

4 Servings

Ingredients
4 4 oz pieces of salmon
Salt and pepper
1 bunch of cilantro
2 tbsp toasted pine nuts
¼ cup olive oil
4 cloves garlic
1 tbsp fresh lime juice
¼ cup grated parmesan cheese

Directions
1. Get immersion circulator setup and start preheating water bath to 115 degrees F (or temp of your choice from page 73).
2. Season the salmon with the salt and pepper.
3. Add the fish to your bag of choice (page 9). Seal the bag and remove the air using your method of choice. Drop the bag into the water bath. Cook for 45 minutes - 1 hour.
4. While the salmon is cooking, add remaining ingredients to a food processor. Blend until mostly smooth.
5. When done cooking, remove fish from bag.
6. Spread about 1 tbsp of the pesto evenly over each piece of fish. Reserve remaining pesto for use in other dishes - make sure to refrigerate it!

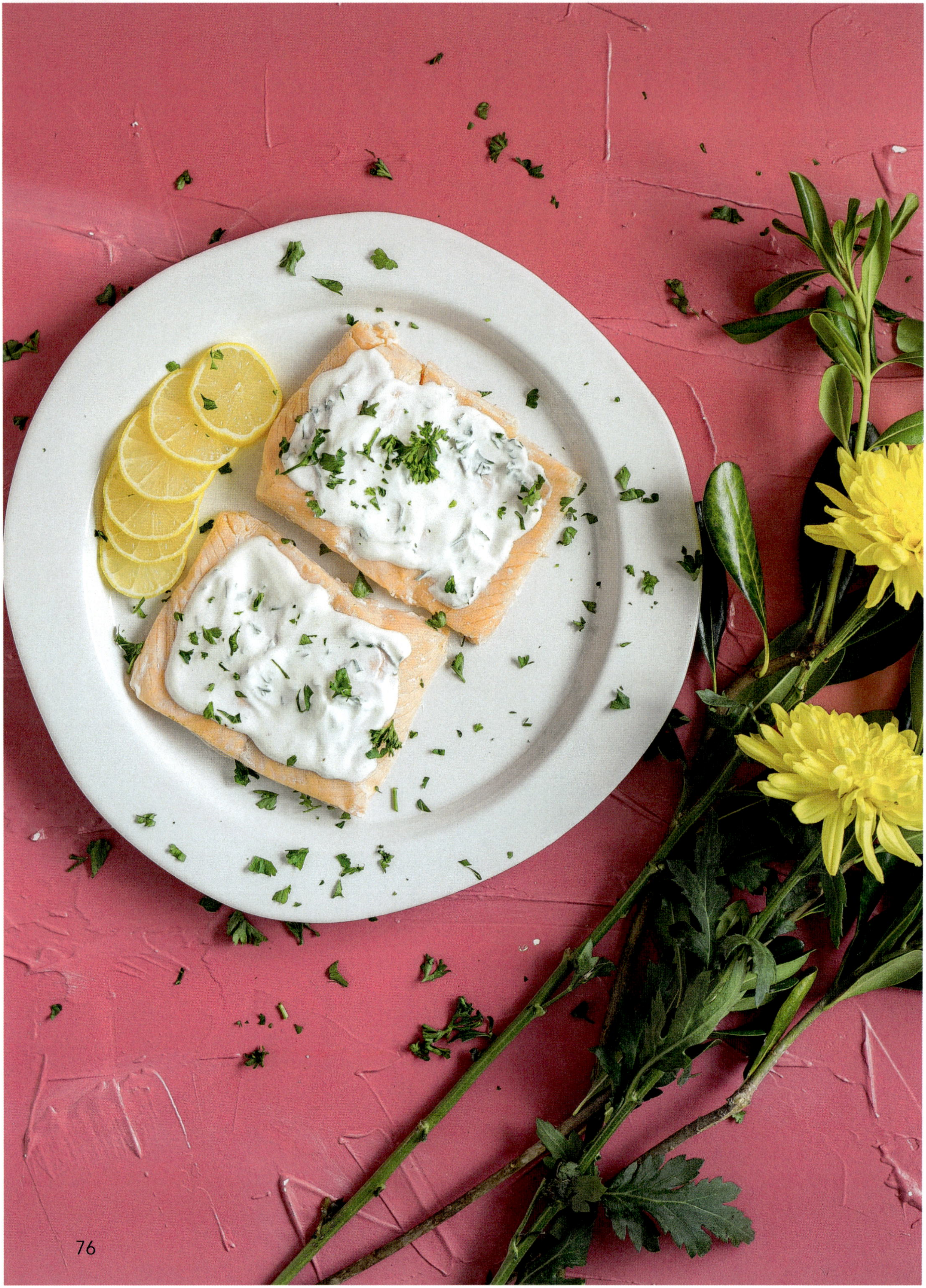

Creamy Ginger Horseradish SALMON

Ready for a salmon topping that packs a punch? We're talkin' a one-two, over here. One: the horseradish. You know about horseradish. The weird, spicy root that will make you cough if you inhale it. Two: ginger. Another potent root with one of the most distinct flavors around. The way these two pair up to cut the buttery salmon will make you swoon.

4 Servings

Ingredients
4 4 oz pieces of salmon
Salt and pepper
½ plain nonfat Greek yogurt
2 tsp prepared horseradish (add more if desired for more of a kick)
1 tsp fresh grated ginger
1 tbsp fresh chopped parsley

Directions
1. Get immersion circulator setup and start preheating water bath to 115 degrees F (or temp of your choice from page 73).
2. Season the salmon with the salt and pepper.
3. Add the fish to your bag of choice (page 9). Seal the bag and remove the air using your method of choice. Drop the bag into the water bath. Cook for 45 minutes - 1 hour.
4. While the salmon is cooking, add remaining ingredients to a bowl and mix together.
5. When done cooking, remove fish from bag.
6. Spread about 1 tbsp of the sauce evenly over each piece of fish. Reserve remaining sauce for use in other dishes - make sure to refrigerate it!

HARISSA

Ingredients
2 red bell peppers, halved and seeded
6 jalapeno peppers
1 habanero pepper
2 tablespoons vegetable oil
1/4 teaspoon caraway seeds
1/4 teaspoon coriander seeds
1/2 teaspoon ground cumin
1/2 teaspoon dried mint
1 teaspoon kosher salt, or to taste
4 garlic cloves, peeled
Juice of 1 lemon
1 tablespoon extra-virgin olive oil

Directions
1. Preheat your oven's broiler and set the oven rack at about 6 inches from the top. Line a baking sheet with aluminum foil.
2. Place red bell peppers with cut sides down onto the prepared baking sheet. Cook under the preheated broiler until the skin of the peppers has blackened and blistered, 5 to 8 minutes. Place the blackened peppers into a bowl and tightly seal with plastic wrap. Allow the peppers to steam as they cool, about 20 minutes.
3. Add the coriander and caraway seeds to a skillet over medium heat. Cook until fragrant, about 2 minutes.
4. Transfer all spices to a blender and add roasted bell peppers, chiles, garlic, lemon juice, and vegetable oil; puree until smooth.
5. Drizzle in extra-virgin olive oil at the end, blending for just a few seconds.

Harissa Orange SALMON

Are you familiar with harissa? Honestly, I wasn't until I stumbled upon it at Trader Joe's. And since I buy all of their condiments and sauces whether or not I know what they are, this little red jar came home with me. On a whim, I slathered it on salmon. It was a good whim. Harissa on salmon paired with fragrant orange is a dream come true.

4 Servings

Ingredients
4 4 oz pieces of salmon
Salt and pepper
2 tbsp harissa sauce (buy a prepared sauce or see recipe on left)
Zest of one orange
Juice of one orange

Directions
1. Get sous vide setup and start preheating water to 115 degrees F (or temp of your choice from page 73).
2. Season the salmon with the salt and pepper. Sprinkle orange zest evenly over salmon pieces.
3. Add the fish to your bag of choice (page 9). Seal the bag and remove the air using your method of choice. Drop the bag into the water bath. Cook for 45 minutes - 1 hour.
4. While the salmon is cooking, add harissa and orange juice to a bowl and mix together.
5. When done cooking, remove fish from bag.
6. Spread about 1 tbsp of the harissa mixture evenly over each piece of fish. Serve.

Hot tip: Save yourself the trouble and and buy the harissa at Trader Joe's! Or don't. Check out the recipe to the left in case you're in a serious DIY mood.

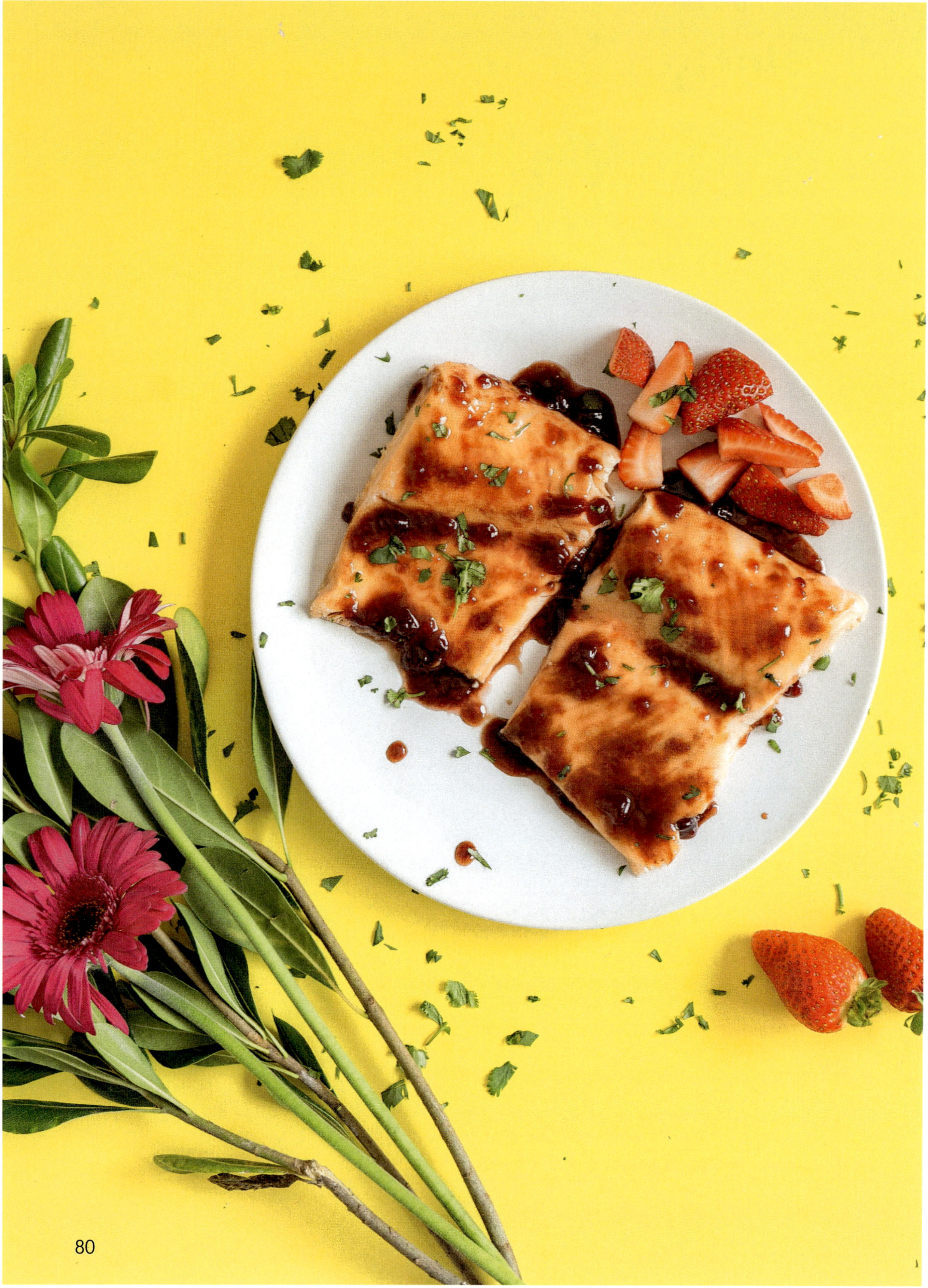

Strawberry Balsamic GLAZED SALMON

I think salmon pairs best with big, bright flavors. Most people agree. But vinegars sometimes get forgotten about in the "bright" flavor category. Balsamic vinegar and salmon pair so well together, especially when you throw in something sweet, like strawberry.

4 Servings

Ingredients
4 4 oz pieces of salmon
Salt and pepper
¼ cup strawberry marmalade
1 ½ tbsp balsamic vinegar
1 tbsp chopped cilantro

Directions
1. Get immersion circulator setup and start preheating water bath to 115 degrees F (or temp of your choice from page 73).
2. Season the salmon with the salt and pepper. Set aside.
3. In a bowl, mix together remaining ingredients.
4. Spread about 1 tbsp of the mixture onto each piece of fish. Save the rest of the sauce for later, wrap, and place in fridge.
5. Add the fish to your bag of choice.
6. Seal the bag and remove the air using water displacement method. Drop the bag into the water bath. Cook for 45 minutes - 1 hour.
7. Remove fish from bag and serve with additional sauce drizzled over the top.

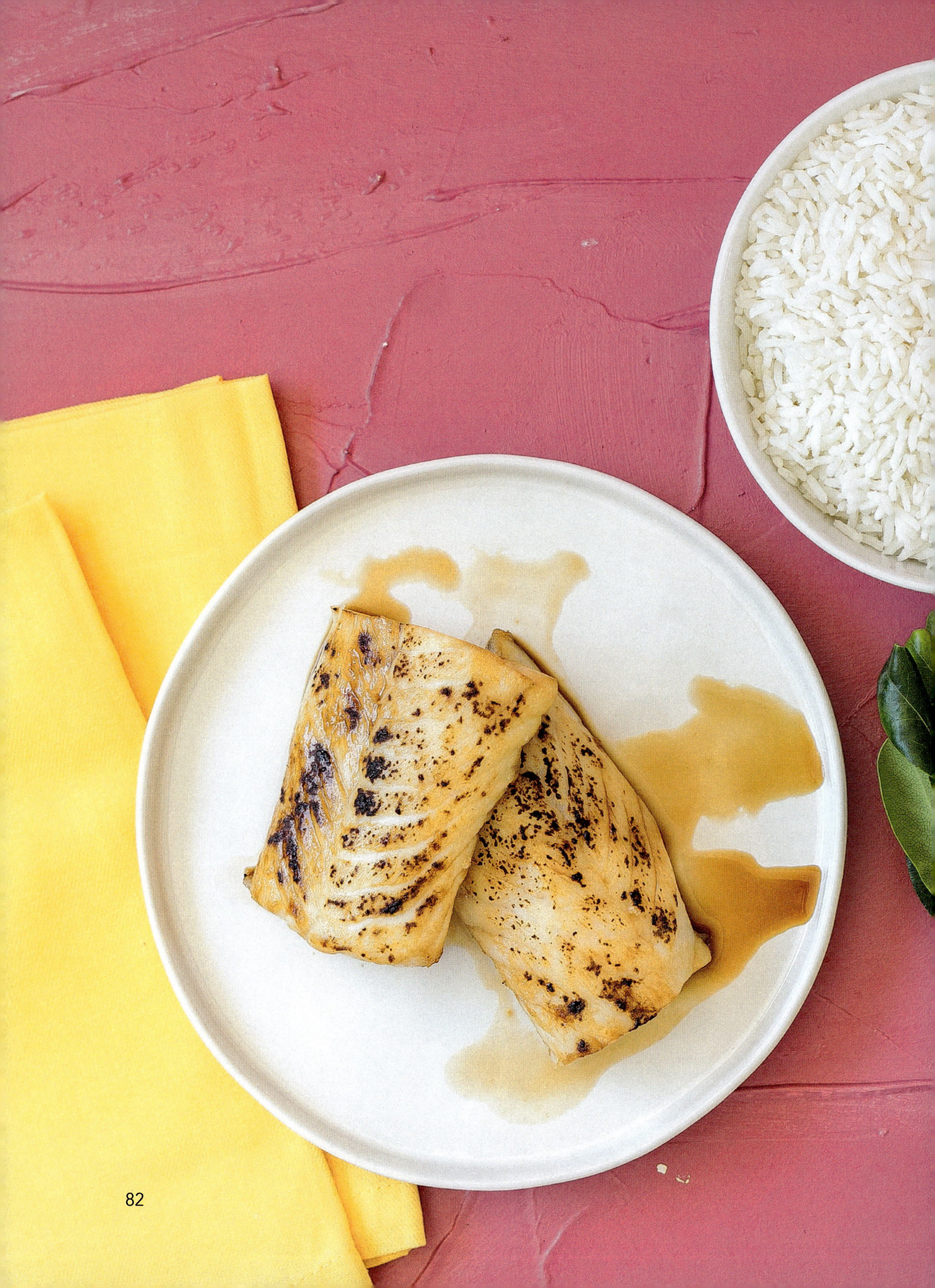

White Fish

It grinds my gears when people tell me they "don't like seafood". There are lots of different seafoods, and they all taste different from each other. And hey, there's a good chance your taste buds have changed since you last tried seafood at 9 years old. Oops, too mean?

Anywho, if you think you don't love seafood, white fish is a great place to start. It is the chicken of the sea (#sorrynotsorry). It's mild, flaky, and takes on the flavor of whatever you top it with. It is super versatile, and totally delicious.

Unlike chicken, fish is less forgiving if you overcook it. It can get tough and stringy and enter into bizarre texture land (hey, maybe this is why people think they don't like fish?). Enter: sous vide! As you know by now, with the help of our friend sous vide, you aren't going to overcook this fish.

These recipes call for cod, but I'm going to let you in on a little secret: nearly any white fish will work well in these recipes. I'm talking cod, halibut, pollock, hake, whatever the fishmonger is slingin' that day (that's ideally tasty AND sustainable).

For several of these recipes, you'll use the water displacement method to get the air out of your bag because there's so much liquid. See page 10 for instructions using the water displacement method.

As we've discussed, you don't want food hanging out in the water bath longer than 3 hours if you're cookin' lower than 130 degrees F. White fish gets to swim for 45 minutes to an hour, so we're allowed to live dangerously, here.

Rare *(just starting to flake, near raw)*   120 degrees F
Medium *(moist and flaky)*   129 degrees F
Well-Done *(moist, flaky, but nearing tough)*   138 degrees F

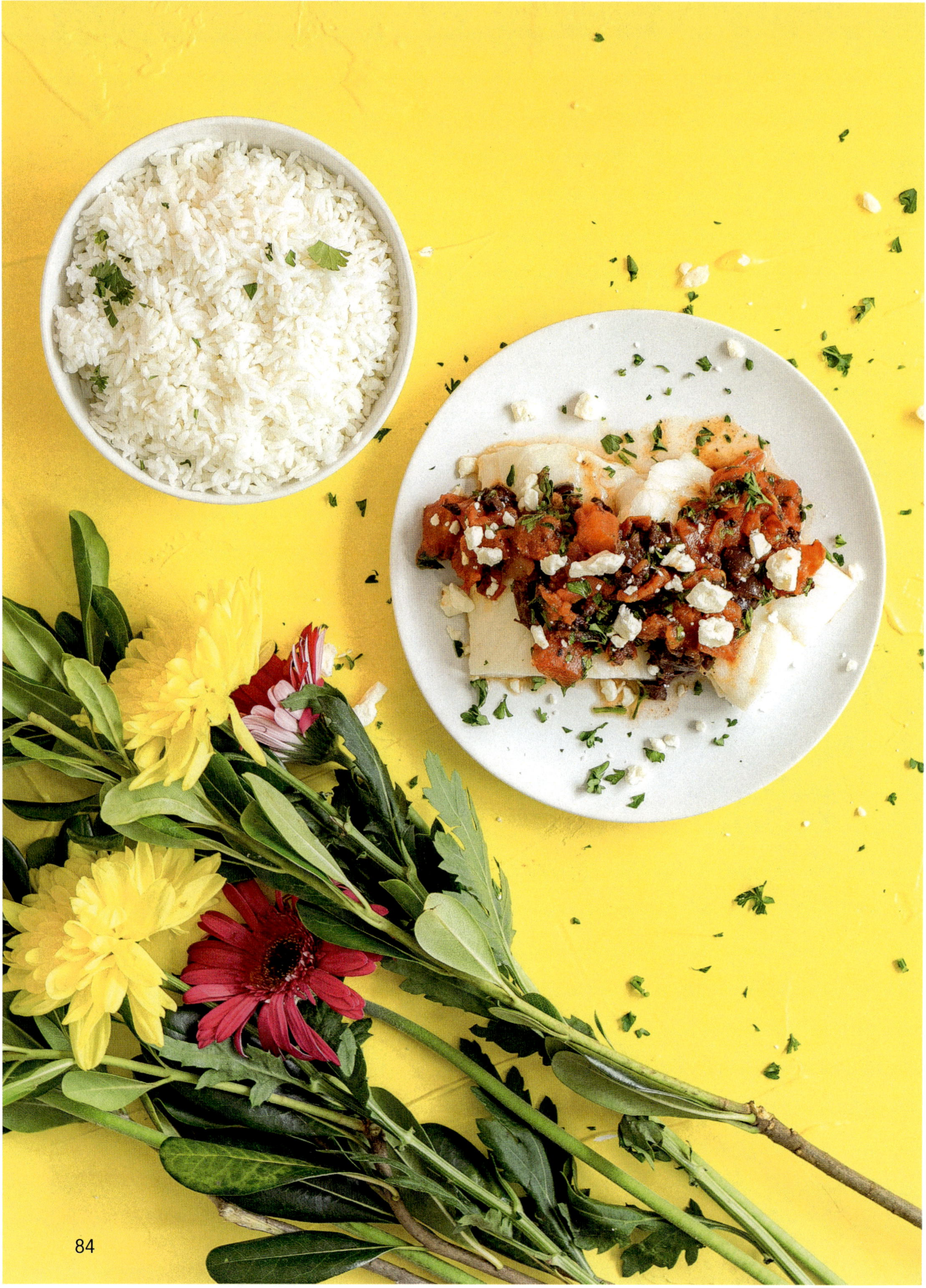

GREEK WHITE FISH

This is a recipe I wrote years ago, and it's been making regular appearances ever since. It was good before I got the sous vide… but now it's great. Before, it got about 10 minutes in the sauce before it was time to serve. Which is fine. But thanks to sous vide, I can let it hang out and absorb all those delicious flavors for a full 45 minutes, turning the flavor level up.

4 Servings

Ingredients
4 4 oz pieces cod (or other white fish)
Salt and pepper
1 tbsp olive oil
1/4 cup diced red onion
1/2 tsp minced garlic
1 14.5 oz can diced tomatoes (try fire roasted!)
2 tbsp chopped sun dried tomatoes
2 tbsp chopped kalamata olives
¼ cup crumbled feta cheese, for serving
Chopped parsley, for garnish

Directions
1. Get immersion circulator setup and start preheating water bath to 129 degrees F (or temp of your choice from page 83).
2. Season the cod with salt and pepper. Set aside.
3. In a small saucepan, heat the olive oil over medium heat.
4. Add the onion and garlic and cook for about 5 minutes, until softened.
5. Add the diced tomatoes, sun dried tomatoes, and kalamata olives. Cook for about 5 minutes, then remove from heat. Let cool for 10 minutes.
6. Add the cod to your bag of choice. Pour tomato sauce into the bag. Remove the air from the bag using the water displacement method.
7. Drop the bag into the water bath. Cook for 30 - 45 minutes.
8. Remove from the bag and serve. Top with feta cheese and chopped parsley.

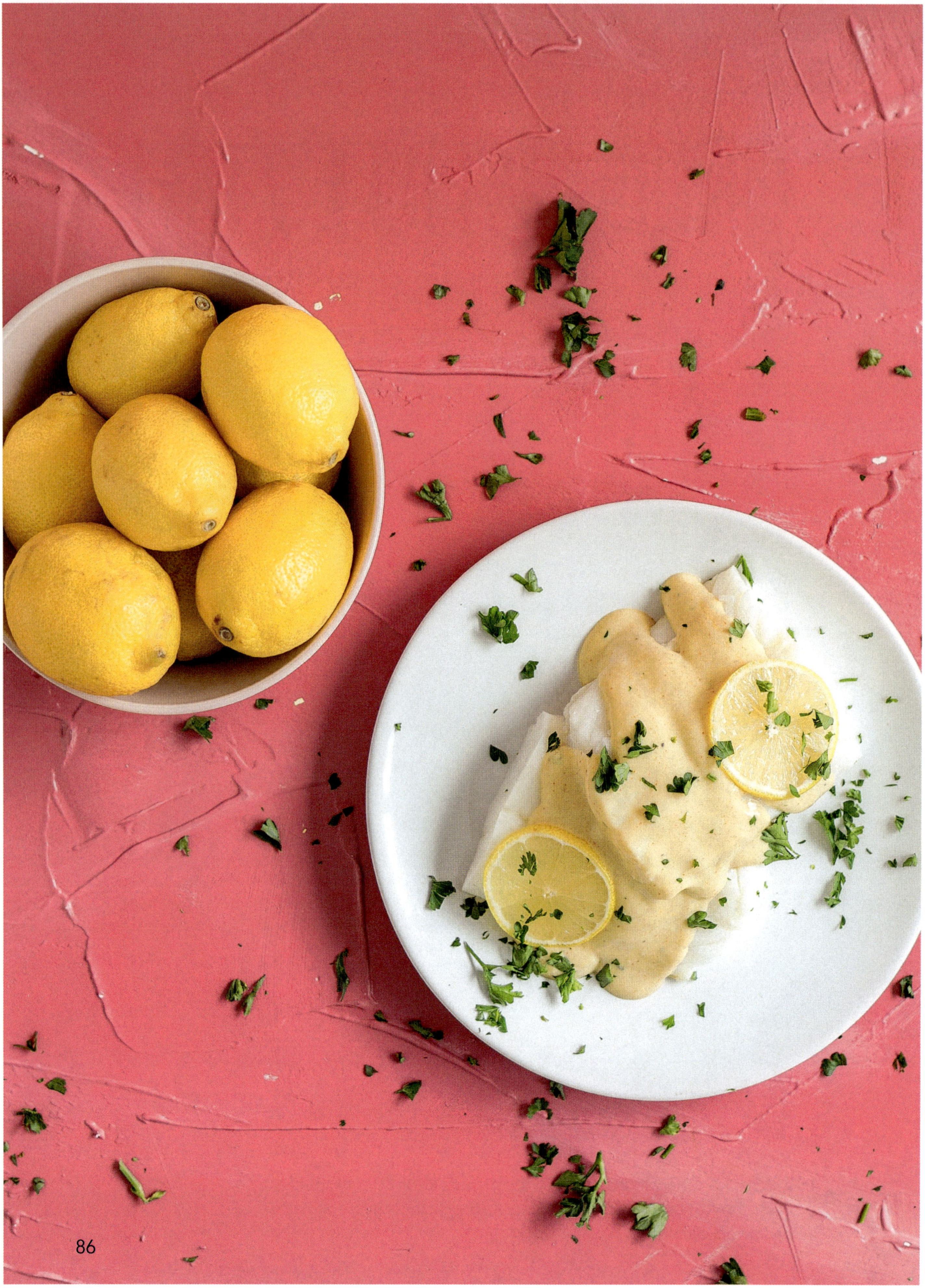

Lemon Dijon WHITE FISH

I got my dad's palette. Is it briny? Is it tangy? Is it full of umami? Then it's for me. One of the easiest ways to drum up these flavors is with a little lemon and a little dijon, especially over a blank canvas like cod. I went for extra credit in this recipe with a creamy sauce, so this one is foolproof. I love this recipe served with roasted, crispy potatoes.

4 Servings

Ingredients
Fish:
4 4 oz pieces of wild Alaskan cod (or other white fish)
Salt
Pepper
Italian seasoning (or other herb blend)
1 - 2 tbsp dijon mustard
2 tbsp cold butter, sliced into thin slices
Lemon, sliced

Sauce:
¼ cup sour cream
2 tbsp dijon mustard
Juice of one lemon (or 1 tbsp lemon juice)
Zest of one lemon
¼ tsp salt
A few grinds of pepper

Chopped parsley for garnish (optional)

Directions
1. Get immersion circulator setup and start preheating water bath to 129 degrees F (or temp of your choice from page 83).
2. Season the cod with the salt, pepper, and Italian seasoning. Rub dijon mustard evenly over each piece of fish.
3. Add the fish to your bag of choice. Evenly distribute the butter and lemon slices over the fish in the bags.
4. Seal the bag and remove the air using your desired method. Drop the bag into the water bath. Cook for 30 - 45 minutes.
5. While the fish is cooking, prepare the sauce. In a small saucepan over low heat, mix together all ingredients for sauce. Stir frequently until sour cream has warmed through and all ingredients are combined. Remove from heat.
6. Remove fish from bag and serve with sauce drizzled over it.

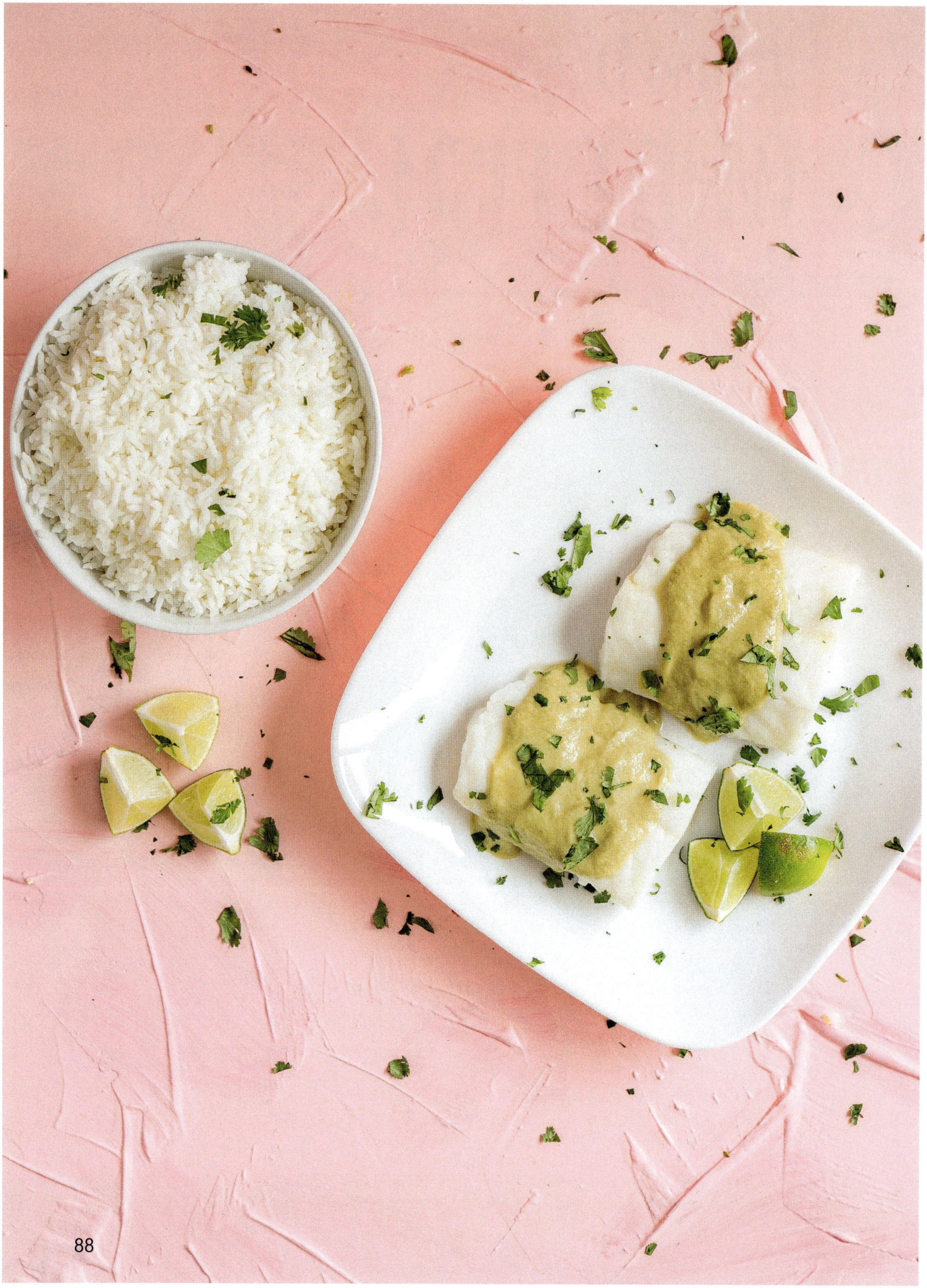

Thai Green Curry WHITE FISH

Thai Green Curry is one of my favorite things to eat on this earth. The sauce makes a regular appearance in my kitchen, and I'm going to let you in on a secret: sometimes I use a jar from Trader Joe's. Because it's great, and sometimes you need dinner to be easy. Seafood and citrus are such a classic pairing, and the creamy lime flavors really make this dish pop.

4 Servings

Ingredients
4 4 oz pieces of cod (or other white fish)
Salt and pepper
1 tbsp olive oil
½ yellow onion, chopped
1 tbsp Thai green curry paste
1 14 oz can unsweetened coconut milk
Zest of one lime
Juice of 1 lime
½ tsp fish sauce
¼ cup chopped fresh cilantro (reserve 1 tbsp for garnish)
1 tbsp chopped fresh basil

Directions
1. Get immersion circulator setup and start preheating water bath to 129 degrees F (or temp of your choice from page 83).
2. Season the cod with salt and pepper.
3. Add the cod to your bag of choice (page 9). Remove the air from the bag using your method of choice (page 10).
4. Drop the bag into the water bath. Cook for 30 - 45 minutes.
5. While the cod is cooking, prepare the sauce. In a small saucepan, heat the olive oil over medium heat. Add the onion and cook for about 5 minutes, until softened.
6. Add the green curry paste and cook for about 3 minutes, until fragrant.
7. Add the coconut milk, lime zest, lime juice, and fish sauce. Continue cooking, stirring constantly, for about 3 minutes.
8. Remove from heat. Stir in the cilantro and basil.
9. Remove the fish from the bag. Serve the fish over steamed white rice and top with green curry sauce.

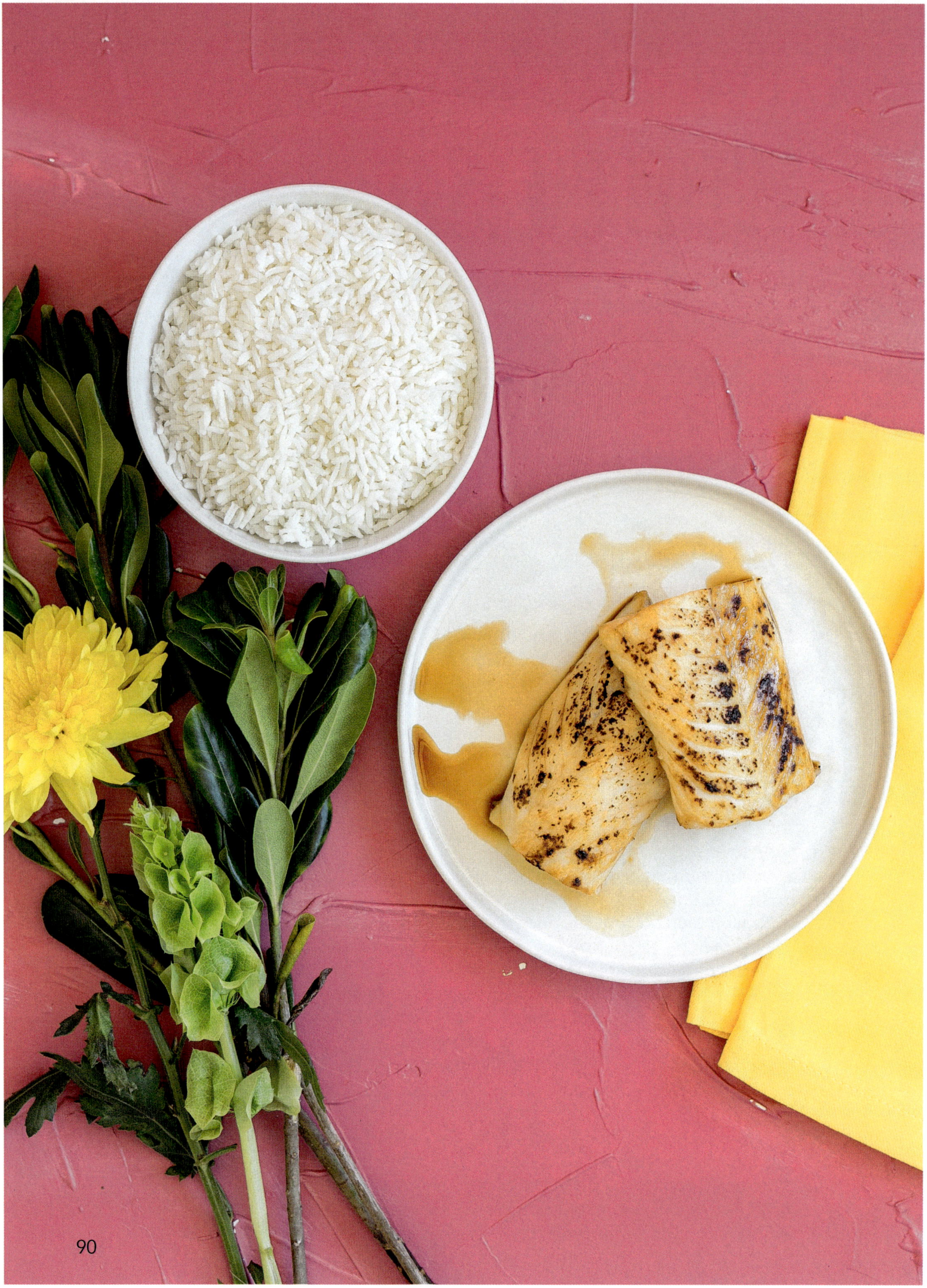

MISO WHITE COD

Can you feel it? That's the hot glare of foodies everywhere staring me down. This recipe traditionally uses black cod, which is oilier, meatier, and frankly, more delicious. But black cod is expensive and hard to come by, so you know what? We're swapping it for your standard cod. This recipe is another umami-laced wonder that's gonna knock your socks off. Pinky swear.

4 Servings

Ingredients
1/4 cup mirin
4 tbsp white miso paste
2 tbsp brown sugar
4 4 oz cod fillets
1 tbsp ghee

Directions
1. Mix together mirin, miso paste, and brown sugar. Rub all over the cod fillets. Add the fish to your bag of choice, seal, and remove the air using your desired method. Place in fridge and let marinate for at least 4 hours, up to 2 days.
2. Get immersion circulator setup and start preheating water bath to 129 degrees F (or temp of your choice from page 83).
3. Drop the bag into the water bath. Cook for 30 - 45 minutes.
4. Preheat a cast iron skillet over high heat. Add ghee to skillet and melt.
5. Remove fish from water bath and bag. Sear in hot skillet on both sides until browned.

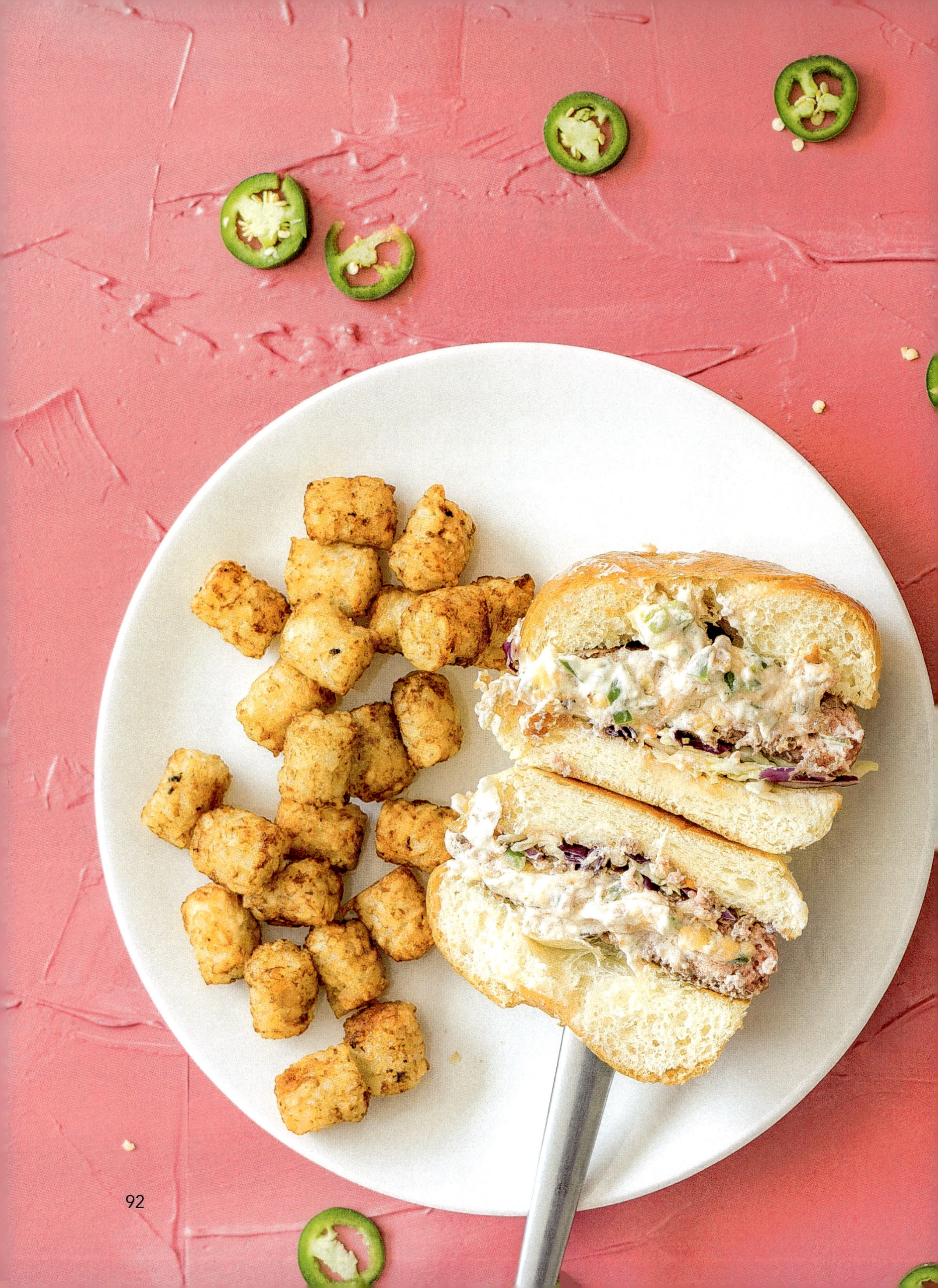

Stuffed Burgers

These stuffed burgers might be the most fun recipes I've ever written. I love burgers. I love a traditional burger with American cheese and pickles. I love a turkey burger with cranberry sauce and blue cheese. I love a burger piled high with all the toppings in the book. But do you know what makes a burger the best it can be? Stuffing all those toppings inside the burger.

The cheese gets melty and gooey in a way that's really difficult to achieve when cooking burgers on a grill without overcooking them because TIME. But we've got time in spades with sous vide.

These burgers are messy, ooey-gooey, and all things right in this world. They come stuffed with enough flavor that I don't think condiments are necessary, but you can add them if you want. The key is a high quality bun, slathered with butter and lightly toasted. Please and thank you.

For these recipes, you'll use the water displacement method to get the air out of your bag so you don't damage the burgers. See page 10 for instructions on using the water displacement method.

I love a medium rare burger, but not all do. Here are some options so you can make the burger of your dreams. My preferred temp is in the safety zone: 130 degrees F. But you can go lower if you want. As we talked about in the beginning of the book, you shouldn't let your food hang out in the water bath longer than 3 hours if you're cookin' lower than 130 degrees F.

Rare *(very pink - just cooked through)* — 125 degrees F
Medium-Rare *(pink all through the middle)* — 130 degrees F
Medium-Well *(just a little pink in the middle)* — 135 degrees F
Well Done *(no pink)* — 145 degrees F

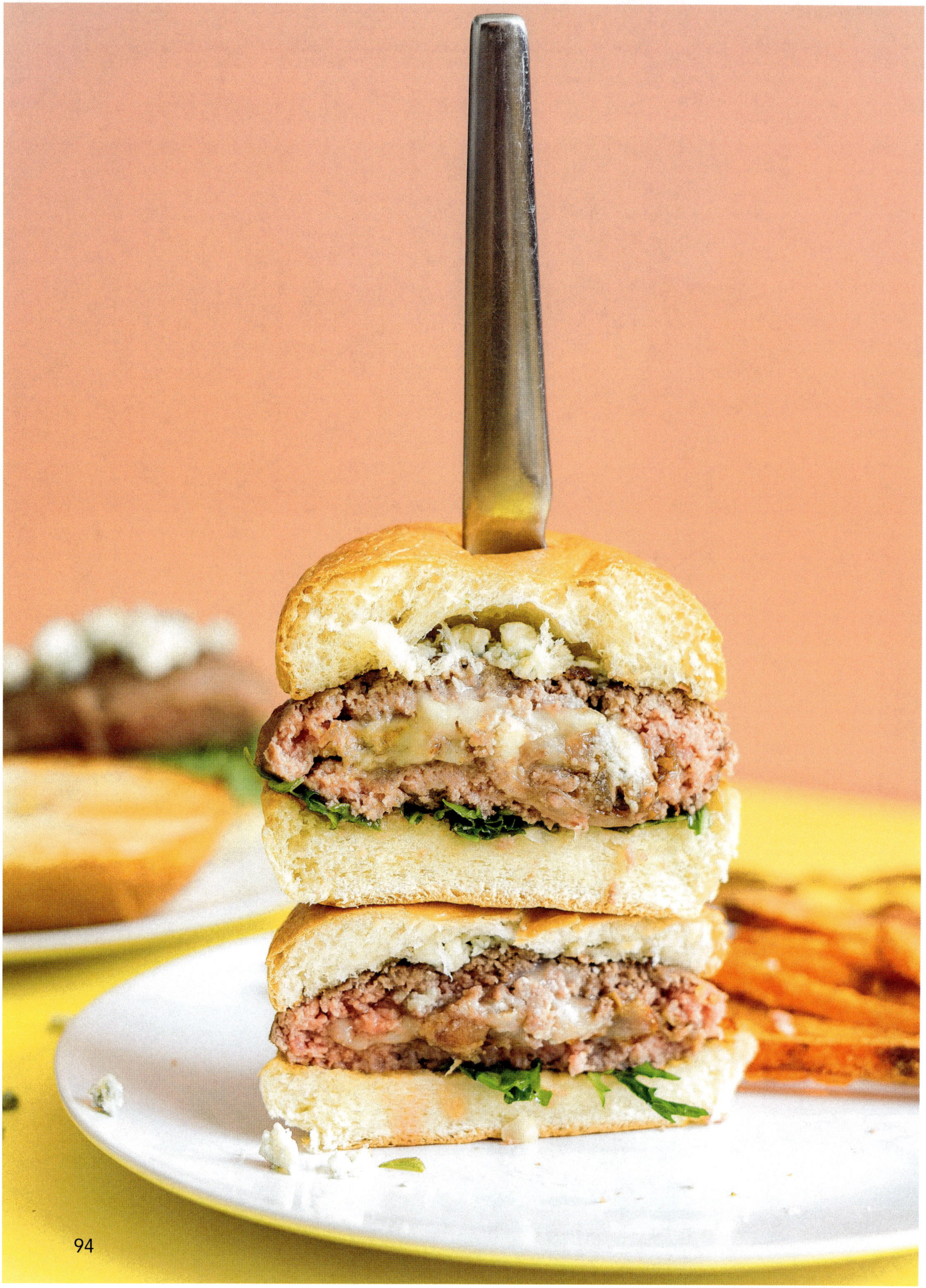

Bacon Blue Cheese Date
STUFFED BURGERS

I am such a sucker for funky-sweet combos, and blue cheese + date is one of my favorites. Any time I see a burger like this on a menu, I feel compelled to order it, and this just doesn't happen often enough. So, I make them at home. And when you're playing with multiple ingredients like this, stuffing the burger mitigates the risk of everything just sliding off as you're eating it. This burger is for PRACTICAL people.

4 Servings

Ingredients
1 pound 85/15 ground beef
2 tsp kosher salt
1 tsp ground black pepper
¼ cup crumbled blue cheese
6 oz pitted dates, chopped
6 slices bacon, crumbled
1 tsp fresh chopped thyme
4 brioche buns

Directions
1. Get immersion circulator setup and start preheating water bath to 130 degrees F (or temp of your choice from page 93).
2. In a large bowl, add the ground beef, salt, and pepper. Mix with your hands until salt and pepper are evenly distributed.
3. Divide the meat into 8 equal sized balls. Press flat into relatively thin circles, just shy of ½ inch.
4. Combine remaining ingredients (except buns) in a small bowl until ingredients are evenly distributed.
5. Spoon a quarter of the blue cheese mixture onto each of four of the patties, leaving about ¾ of an inch around the edge free of blue cheese.
6. Place a patty that hasn't been topped with the blue cheese mixture over the top of one that has. Pinch the edges together and reshape to seal in the other ingredients. Repeat with remaining patties.
7. Add to bag of choice and remove the air using the water displacement method. Add the bag to the water bath and cook for 45 minutes to 2 ½ hours.
8. Preheat a cast iron skillet over high heat. Remove burgers from water bath and bag. Sear in hot skillet on both sides until browned.
9. Let rest on for 5 minutes. Serve on a bun with your favorite toppings.

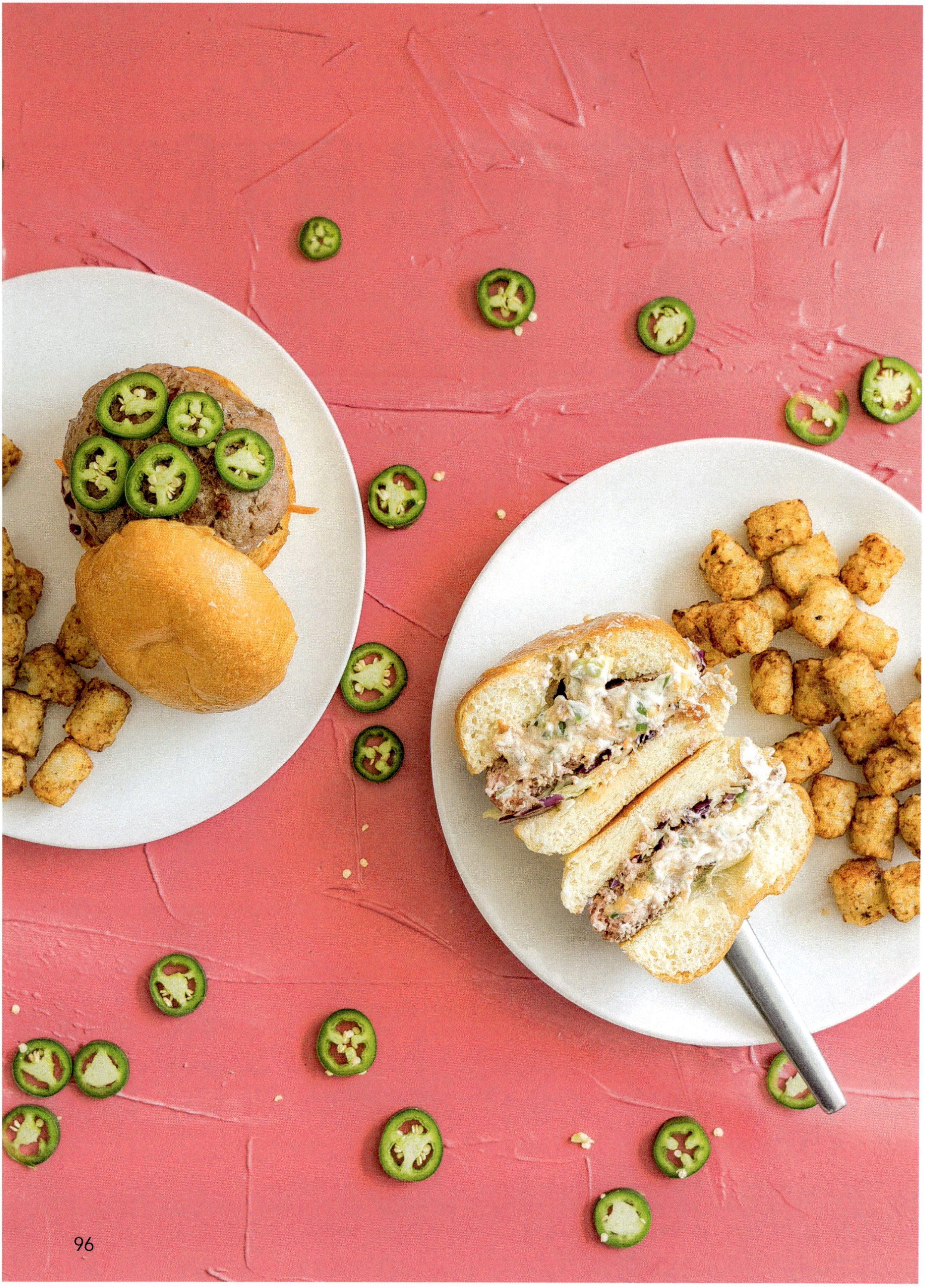

Jalapeño Popper STUFFED BURGERS

I credit my love of jalapeno poppers to my parents, as these are an appetizer go-to at any party they host. They are the perfect combination of creamy, salty and spicy, and they are shockingly addictive. So why not take all of those ingredients, and put them inside a burger? It's an obvious move, and I'm disappointed in myself because it took 27 years for the idea to occur to me.

4 Servings

Ingredients
1 pound 85/15 ground beef
2 tsp kosher salt
1 tsp ground black pepper
1/3 cup cream cheese, softened
¼ cup bacon, crumbled
2 tbsp shredded cheddar cheese
1 jalapeno, seeded and ribs removed, minced
4 brioche buns

Directions
1. Get immersion circulator setup and start preheating water bath to 130 degrees F (or temp of your choice from page 93).
2. In a large bowl, add the ground beef, salt, and pepper. Mix with your hands until salt and pepper are evenly distributed.
3. Divide the meat into 8 equal sized balls. Press flat into relatively thin circles, just shy of ½ inch.
4. Combine remaining ingredients (except buns) in a small bowl.
5. Spoon a quarter of the cream cheese mixture onto each of four of the patties, leaving about ¾ of an inch around the edge free of cream cheese.
6. Place a patty that hasn't been topped with the cream cheese mixture over the top of one that has. Pinch the edges together and reshape to seal in the cheese and bacon. Repeat with remaining patties.
7. Add to bag and remove the air using the water displacement method. Add the bag to the water bath and cook for 45 minutes to 2 ½ hours.
8. Preheat a cast iron skillet over high heat. Remove burgers from water bath and bag. Sear in hot skillet on both sides until browned.
9. Let rest for 5 minutes. Serve on a bun with your favorite toppings.

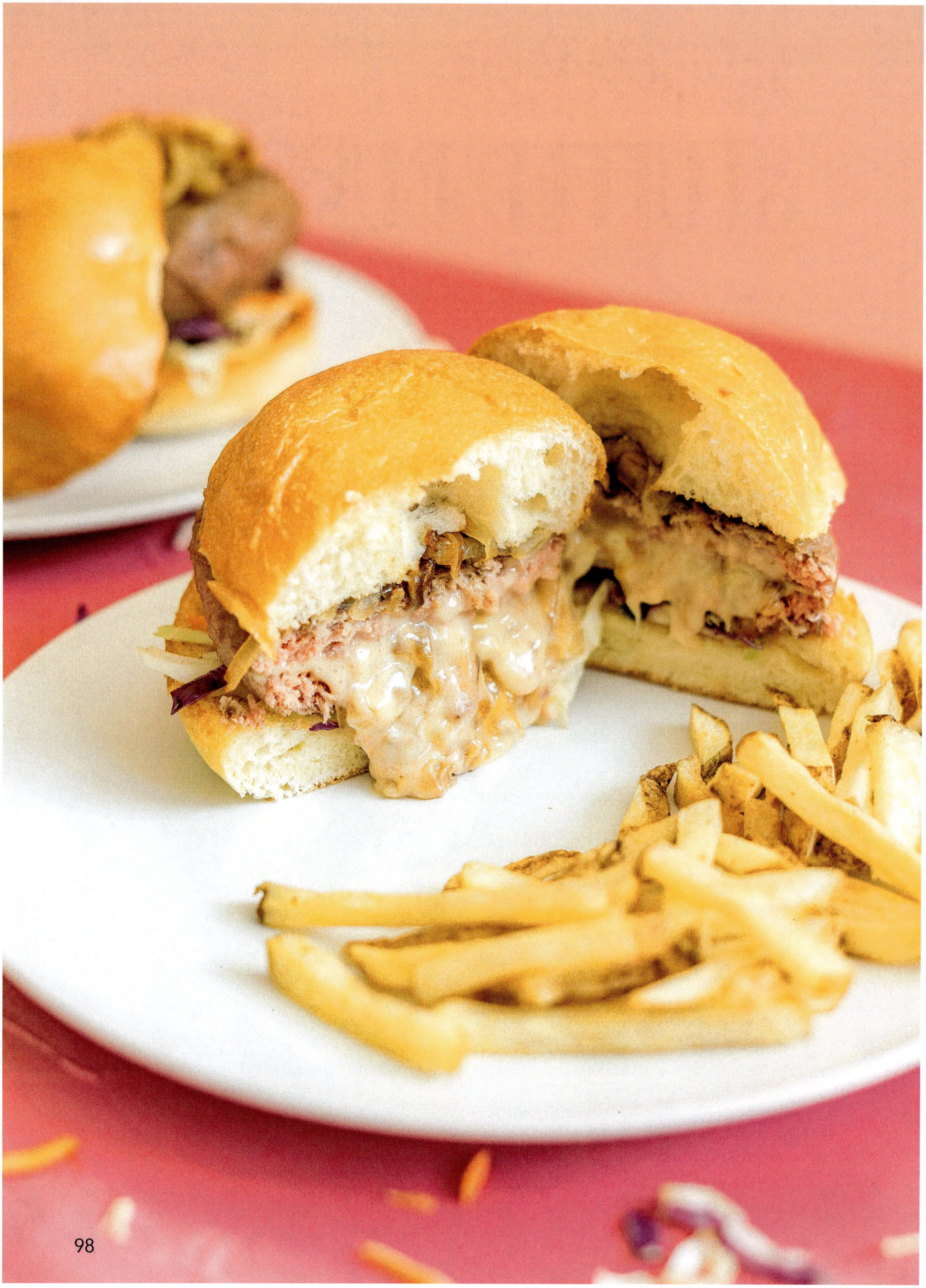

Caramelized Onion Pepper Jack STUFFED BURGERS

Anything with beef gets a level up when you add caramelized onions to it. The sweet smokiness of the onions just complements the beef so well! Throw in gooey, spicy pepper jack, and you've got a winning burger. Pro tip: make a big batch of onions so you have leftovers to throw in Caramelized Onion and Brie Cheese Egg Bites (page 17).

4 Servings

Ingredients
1 pound 85/15 ground beef
2 tsp kosher salt
1 tsp ground black pepper
8 slices pepper jack cheese
1 onion, cut in half long ways and sliced
½ tsp olive oil
4 brioche buns

Directions
1. Get immersion circulator setup and start preheating water bath to 130 degrees F (or temp of your choice from page 93).
2. In a large nonstick skillet, begin heating the olive oil over medium-low heat. Add the sliced onions and cook, stirring occasionally, until soft and golden brown. Adjust the heat as necessary to keep the onions from crisping. This should take about 15 minutes.
3. While the onions are cooking, form the patties. In a large bowl, add the ground beef, salt, and pepper. Mix with your hands until salt and pepper are evenly distributed.
4. Divide the meat into 8 equal sized balls. Press flat into relatively thin circles, just shy of ½ inch.
5. Arrange two slices of pepper jack cheese on each of four of the patties, leaving about ¾ of an inch around the edge free of cheese. You may need to tear the cheese into smaller slices.
7. Top the cheese with enough caramelized onions to form a thin layer.
8. Place a patty that hasn't been topped with the cheese and onions over the top of one that has. Pinch the edges together and reshape to seal in the cheese and onions. Repeat with remaining patties.
9. Add to bag and remove the air using the water displacement method. Add the bag to the water bath and cook for 45 minutes to 2 ½ hours.
10. Preheat a cast iron skillet over high heat. Remove burgers from water bath and bag. Sear in hot skillet on both sides until browned.
11. Let rest for 5 minutes. Serve on a bun with your favorite toppings.

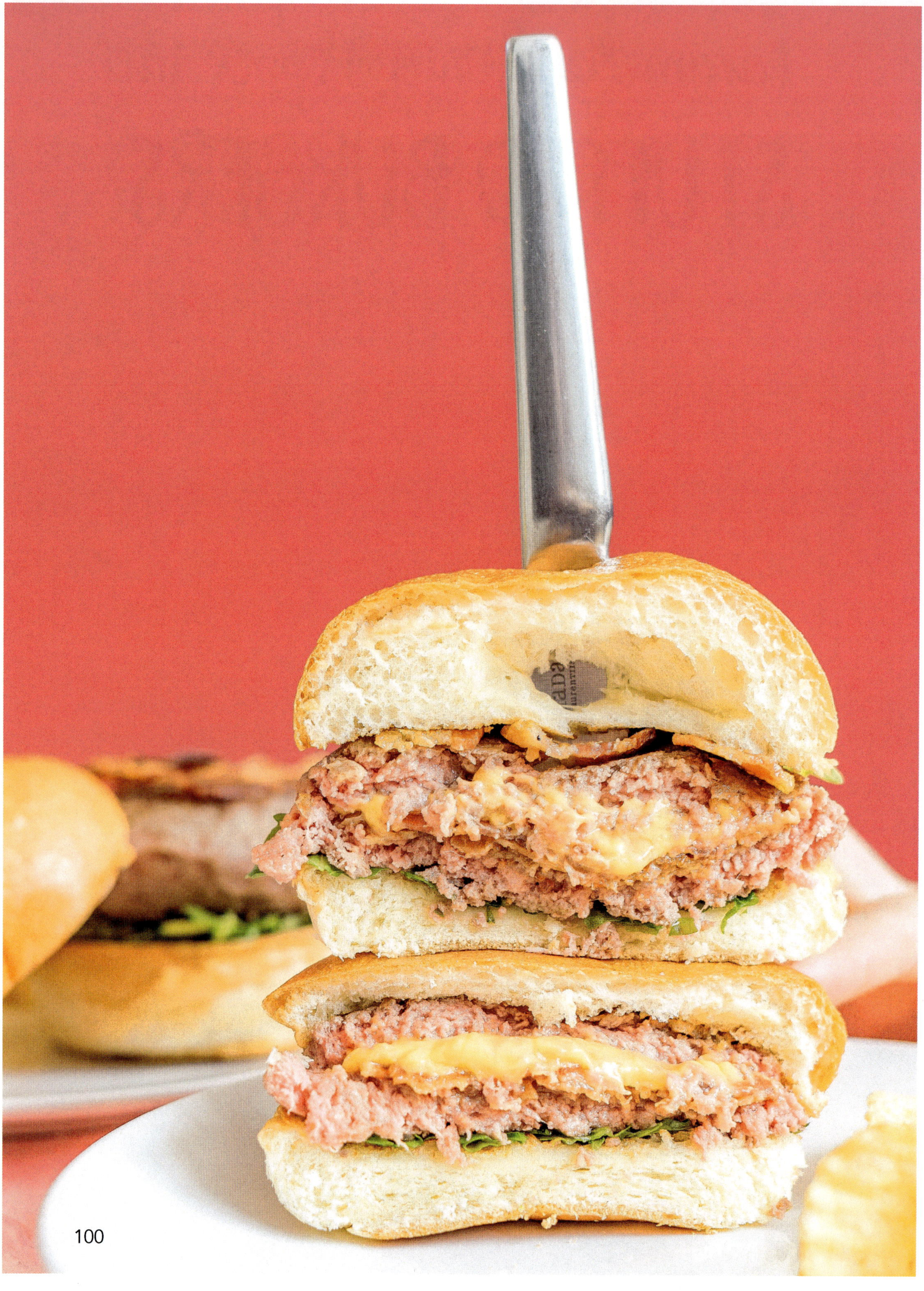

BACON JUICY LUCY

I only learned of the Juicy Lucy's existence a few years ago, and the moment I did, I was determined to find one. Lucky for me, Stormbreaker, one of our favorite local breweries, has a great one on the menu. It was everything I dreamed it would be. It's a burger stuffed with American cheese, and the molten goodness oozes out when you bite into it. It's magical. I took things one step further with this recipe with the addition of bacon. Because... bacon.

4 Servings

Ingredients
1 pound 85/15 ground beef
2 tsp kosher salt
1 tsp ground black pepper
6 slices of American cheese
6 tbsp crumbled, cooked bacon
4 brioche buns

Directions
1. Get immersion circulator setup and start preheating water bath to 130 degrees F (or temp of your choice from page 93).
2. In a large bowl, add the ground beef, salt, and pepper. Mix with your hands until salt and pepper are evenly distributed.
3. Divide the meat into 8 equal sized balls. Press flat into relatively thin circles, just shy of ½ inch.
4. Tear the American cheese into quarters. Place 6 quarters of cheese on one of the burger patties, leaving about ¾ of an inch around the edge free of cheese. Repeat with three more patties.
5. Add about 1 tbsp of crumbled bacon on top of the cheese.
6. Place a patty that hasn't been topped with cheese and bacon over the top of one that has. Pinch the edges together and reshape to seal in the cheese and bacon. Repeat with remaining patties.
7. Add to bag and remove the air using the water displacement method. Add the bag to the water bath and cook for 45 minutes to 2 ½ hours.
8. Preheat a cast iron skillet over high heat. Remove burgers from water bath and bag. Sear in hot skillet on both sides until browned.
9. Let rest on cutting board for 5 minutes. Serve on a bun with your favorite toppings.

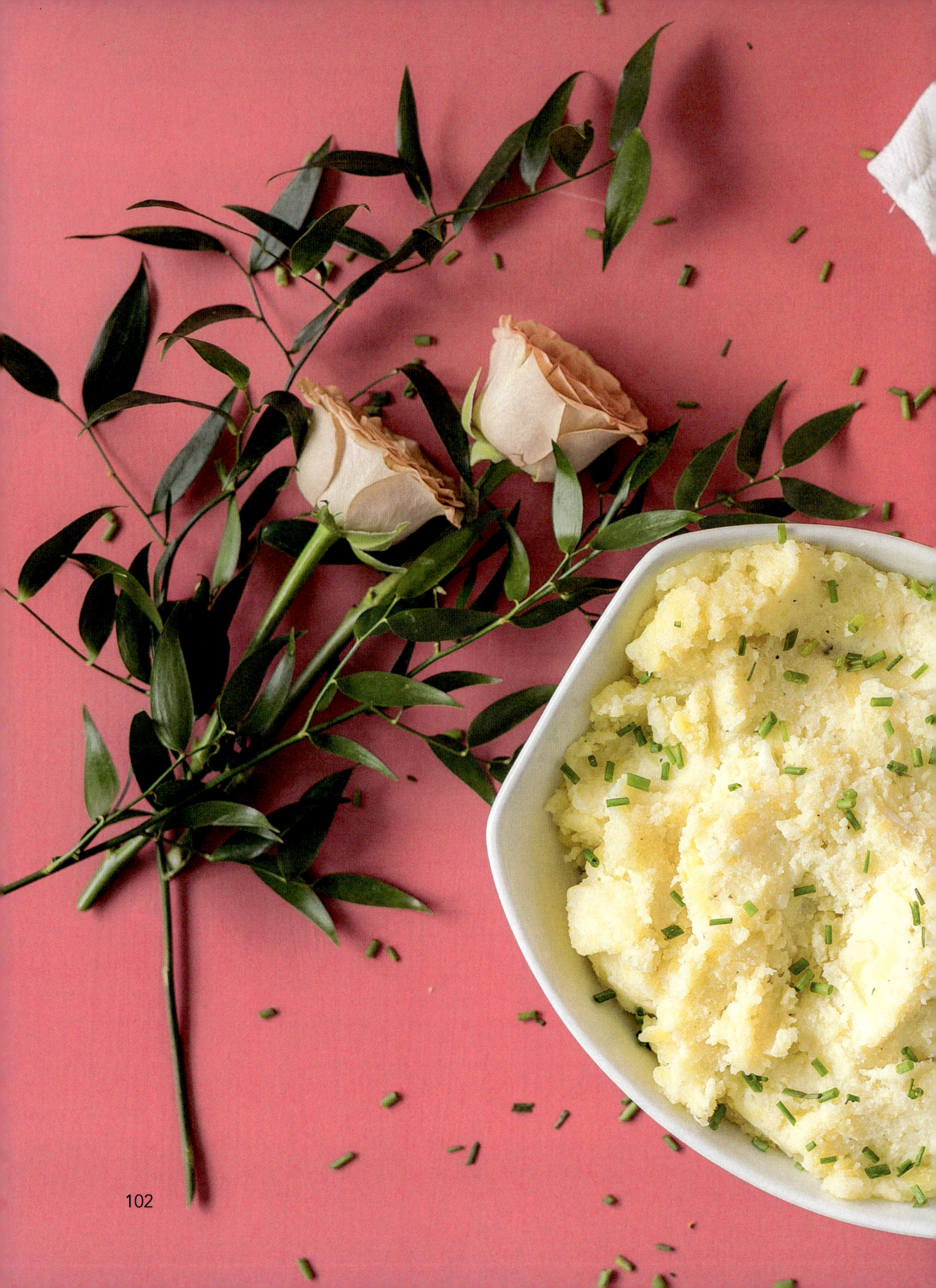

Mashed Roots

Sous vide cooking is usually associated with meat, and for good reason. But just you wait until you use this method for your veggies. Specifically, your mashes. There is nothing so creamy, dreamy, and flavor-packed as these sides. Wanna know why? Instead of cooking in water, you cook the root veggies in ingredients like heavy cream, butter, garlic and ginger, so the roots absorb flavors right into their spongy souls.

And just like all my other recipes, these mashes are going to make your life a thousand times easier, especially when you're feeding a big group. Throw all these ingredients in a bag, put the bag in the bath, then walk away. You aren't even tied to a cooking time, so you've got all the flexibility in the world.

Admittedly, since you are cooking with lots of dairy, these mashes are a bit more indulgent than the standard fare. But life is too short to worry about calories! Right? Right. (Okay, okay, Husband and I typically stick with a boring cauliflower mash. But these sides are our go-to for special occasions.)

For these recipes, you'll use the water displacement method to get the air out of your bag. See page 10 for instructions on using the water displacement method.

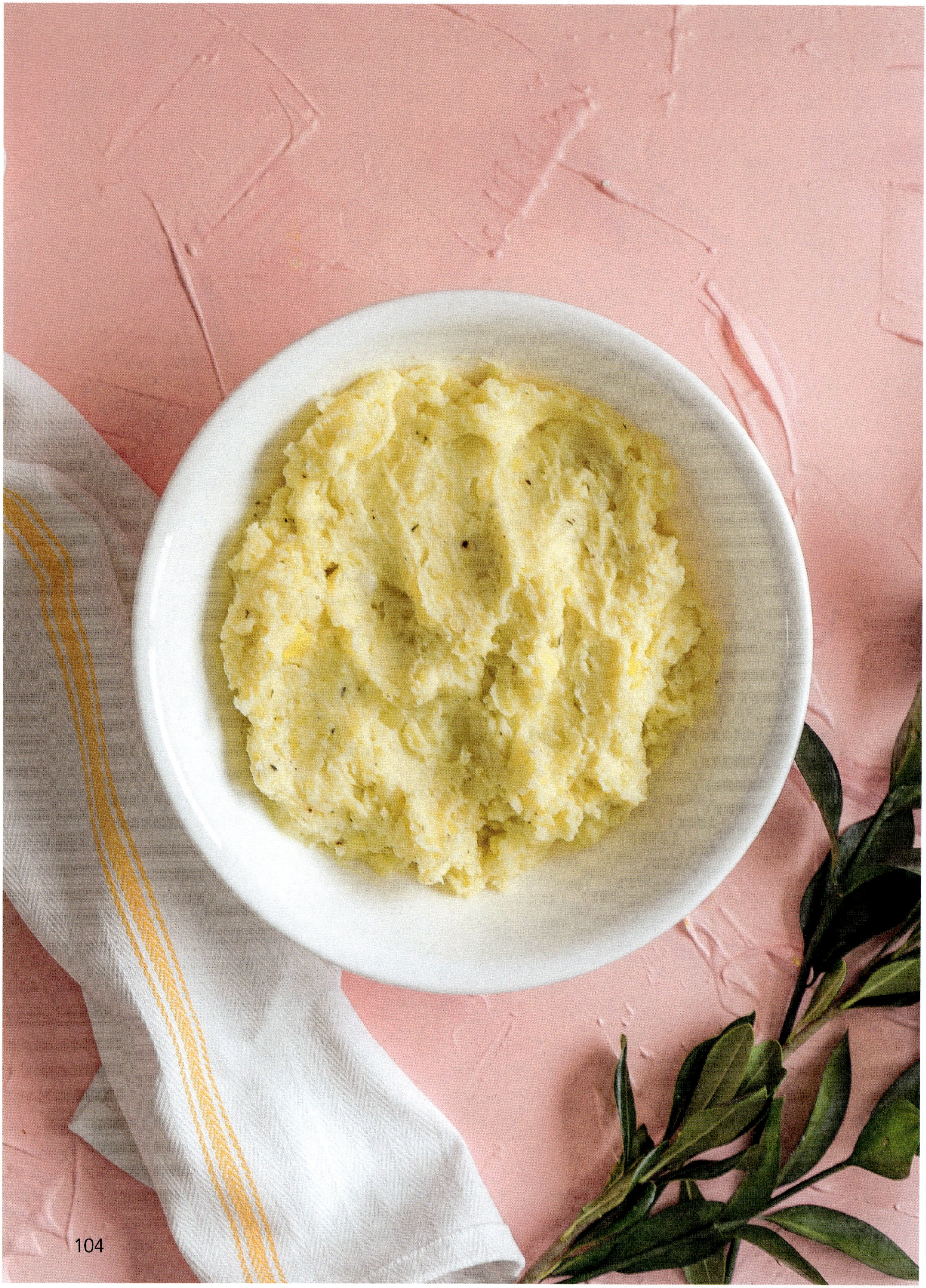

Garlicky MASHED POTATOES

Ready for a weird confession? Mashed potatoes are my favorite food. I could happily eat a huge bowl of them for every meal. The texture, the flavor, everything about them brings me comfort and joy. Husband and I usually swap them for mashed cauliflower, which is good… but not nearly the same. It's especially hard to go back to that lighter alternative after you've had these mashed potatoes.

6 Servings

Ingredients
2 ½ pounds Yukon potatoes, peeled and cut into ¼ inch slices
¾ cup heavy cream
½ cup butter, sliced
7 garlic cloves, smashed
1 tsp salt
½ tsp ground black pepper
2 tsp Italian seasoning (or your favorite salt free herb blend)

Directions
1. Get immersion circulator setup and start preheating water bath to 190 degrees F. This is a hot temperature for sous vide cooking: don't forget to place a trivet under your container!
2. Add all ingredients to your bag of choice and toss to evenly disperse everything. Use the water displacement method (page 10) to remove the air and seal the bag.
3. Drop the bag into the water and make sure the potatoes are completely submerged. Cook for 2 hours, up to 6 hours.
4. Remove the bag from the water. Remove the potatoes from the bag, leaving the liquid behind (but reserve the liquid!) and add to a bowl.
5. Use a potato masher to mash. Stir in liquid a bit at a time and continue mashing until the mash has reached your desired consistency. Taste and season with more salt if desired.

106

Curried BUTTERNUT SQUASH

I love that butternut squash pairs so well with a variety of flavors, and it's got its own earthy sweetness. And you know what those flavors pair oh so well with? Curry. Some people are afraid of curry because they associate with spicy. I call for a mild curry powder here, and if heat ain't for you, just omit the cayenne.

6 Servings

Ingredients
1 3 pound butternut squash, peeled and cubed (about 4 cups of cubes)
½ cup heavy cream
¼ cup butter, sliced
2 tbsp tahini
2 tsp grated ginger
1 tsp salt
1 tsp mild curry powder
¼ tsp cayenne pepper (optional)

Directions
1. Get sous vide setup and start preheating water to 190 degrees F. This is a hot temperature for sous vide cooking: don't forget to place a trivet under your container!
2. Add all ingredients to your bag of choice and toss to evenly disperse everything. Use the water displacement method (page 10) to remove the air and seal the bag.
3. Drop the bag into the water and make sure the squash is completely submerged. Cook for 2 hours, up to 6 hours.
4. Remove the bag from the water. Remove the butternut squash from the bag, leaving the liquid behind (but reserve the liquid!) and add to a bowl.
5. Use a potato masher to mash. Stir in liquid a bit at a time and continue mashing until the mash has reached your desired consistency. Taste and season with more salt if desired.

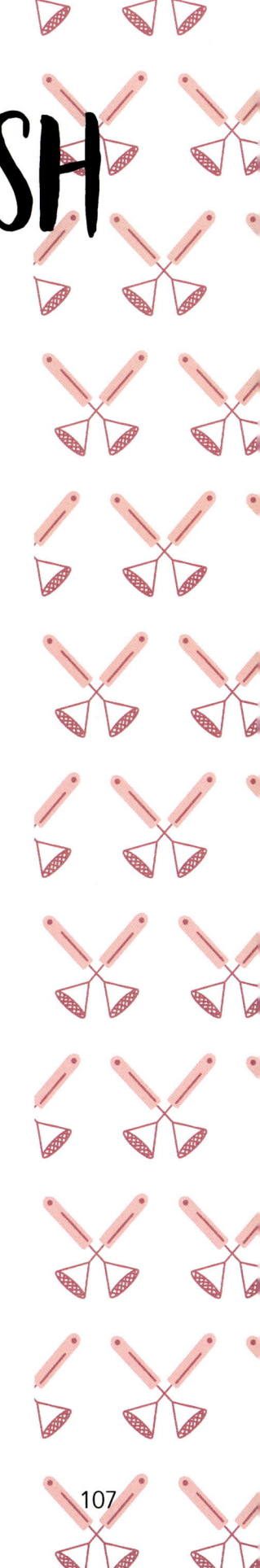

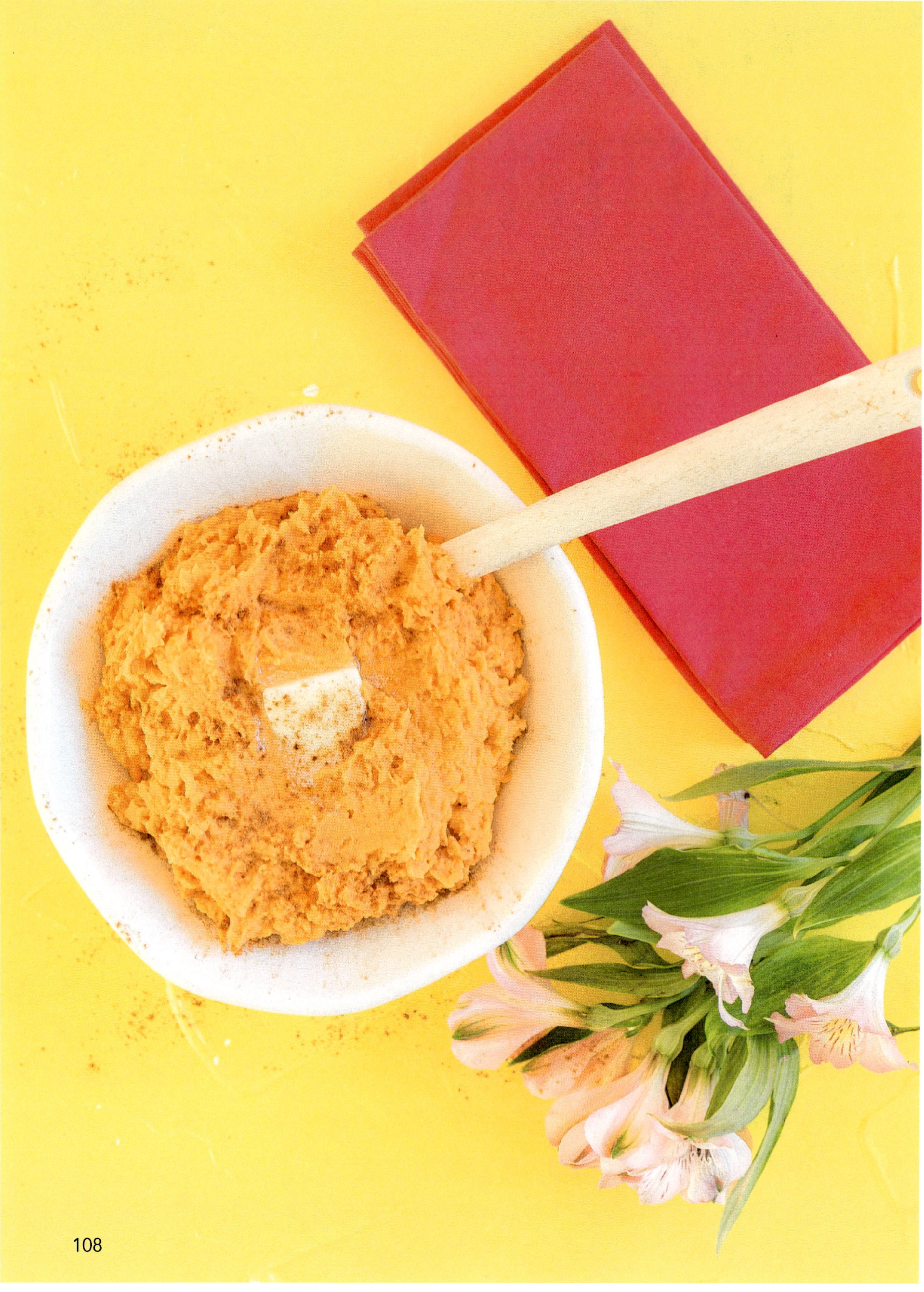

Cinnamon Ginger
SWEET POTATOES

These mashed sweet potatoes are what Thanksgiving dreams are made of, minus the marshmallows. Confession: I've never understood the whole marshmallows on sweet potatoes thing at holidays. Do. Not. Get. My mom and I are both adamantly against it, so when you see mashed sweet potatoes on our tables, this is what they look like. And they're way better.

6 Servings

Ingredients
3 large orange sweet potatoes, peeled and cut into ¼ inch rounds
½ cup heavy cream
¼ cup butter, sliced
2 tsp grated ginger
1 tsp salt
2 tsp pumpkin pie spice

Directions
1. Get immersion circulator setup and start preheating water bath to 190 degrees F. This is a hot temperature for sous vide cooking: don't forget to place a trivet under your container!
2. Add all ingredients to your bag of choice and toss to evenly disperse everything. Use the water displacement method (page 10) to remove the air and seal the bag.
3. Drop the bag into the water and make sure the potatoes are completely submerged. Cook for 2 hours, up to 6 hours.
4. Remove the bag from the water. Remove the sweet potatoes from the bag, leaving the liquid behind (but reserve the liquid!) and add to a bowl.
5. Use a potato masher to mash. Stir in liquid a bit at a time and continue mashing until the mash has reached your desired consistency. Taste and season with more salt if desired.

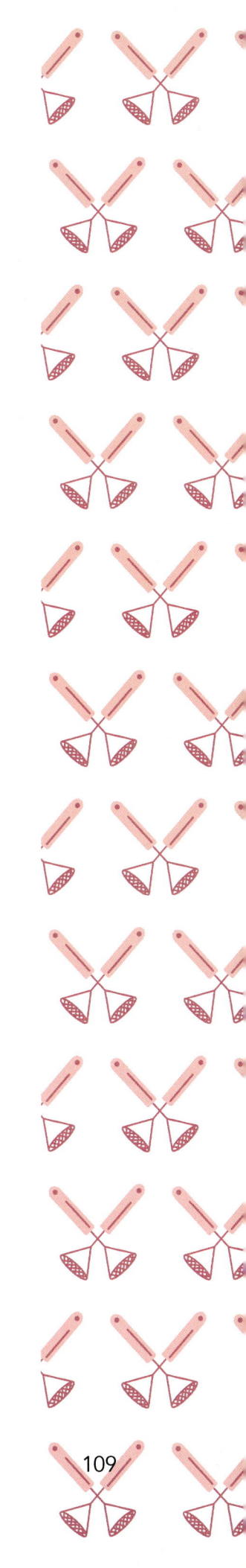

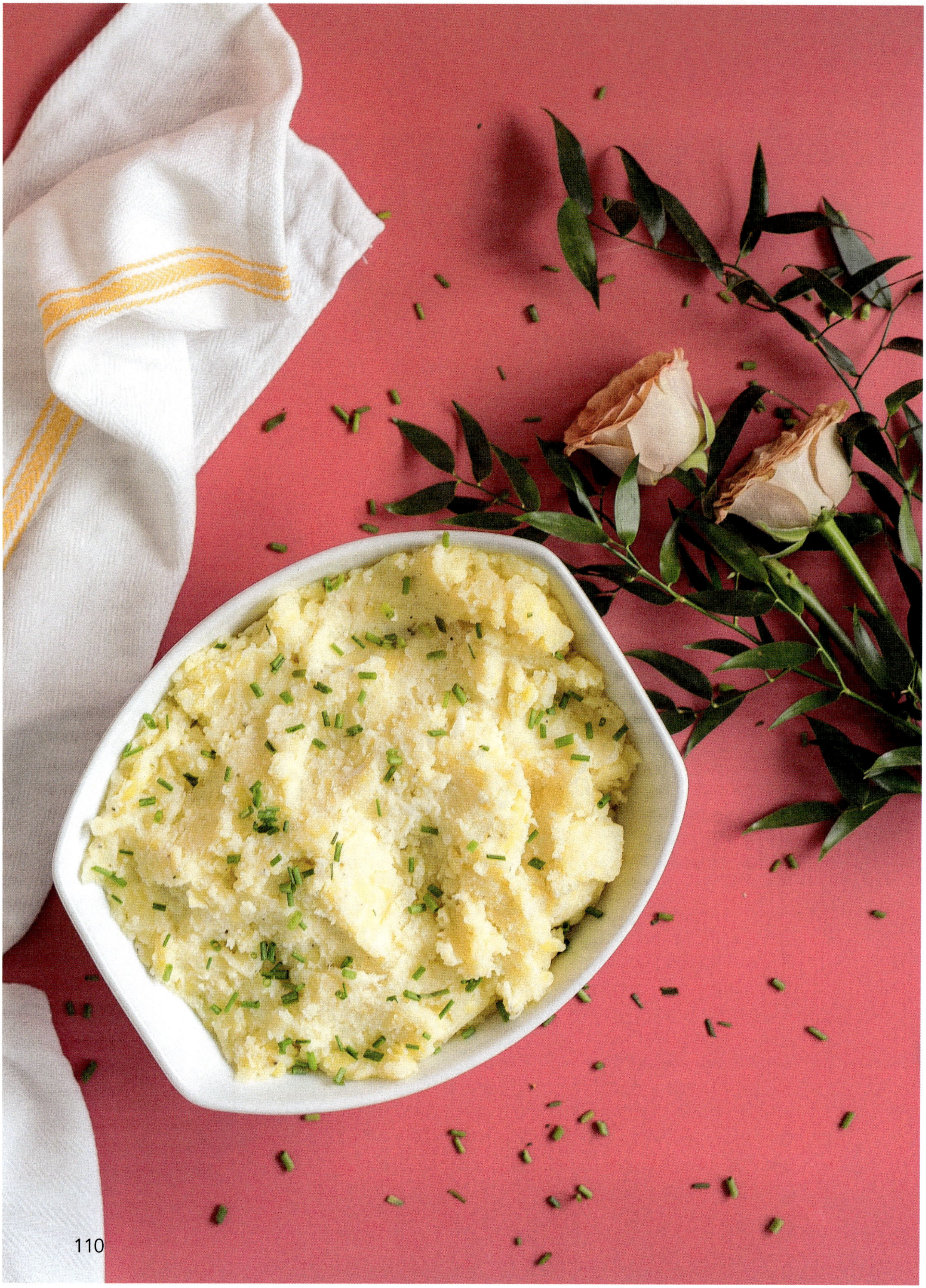

Cream Cheese and Chive PARSNIPS

Parsnips are a lesser used cousin of the carrot, and we've collectively done them a disservice by not putting them to better use. That ends here. Unlike carrots, parsnips aren't particularly sweet and have more of a mild, almost spiced flavor. Add a bunch of tangy cream cheese and oniony chives, and you've got yourself a winning side dish.

6 Servings

Ingredients
10 parsnips, peeled and cubed
¼ cup heavy cream
4 oz cream cheese
¼ cup butter, sliced
1 tsp salt
¼ tsp ground black pepper
1 tsp Italian seasoning (or your favorite salt-free dried herb blend)
1 tbsp chopped chives

Directions
1. Get immersion circulator setup and start preheating water bath to 190 degrees F. This is a hot temperature for sous vide cooking: don't forget to place a trivet under your container!
2. Add all ingredients to your bag of choice and toss to evenly disperse everything. Use the water displacement method (page 10) to remove the air and seal the bag.
3. Drop the bag into the water and make sure the turnips are completely submerged. Cook for 2 hours, up to 6 hours.
4. Remove the bag from the water. Remove the parsnips from the bag, leaving the liquid behind (but reserve the liquid!) and add to a bowl.
5. Use a potato masher to mash. Stir in liquid a bit at a time and continue mashing until the mash has reached your desired consistency. Taste and season with more salt if desired.

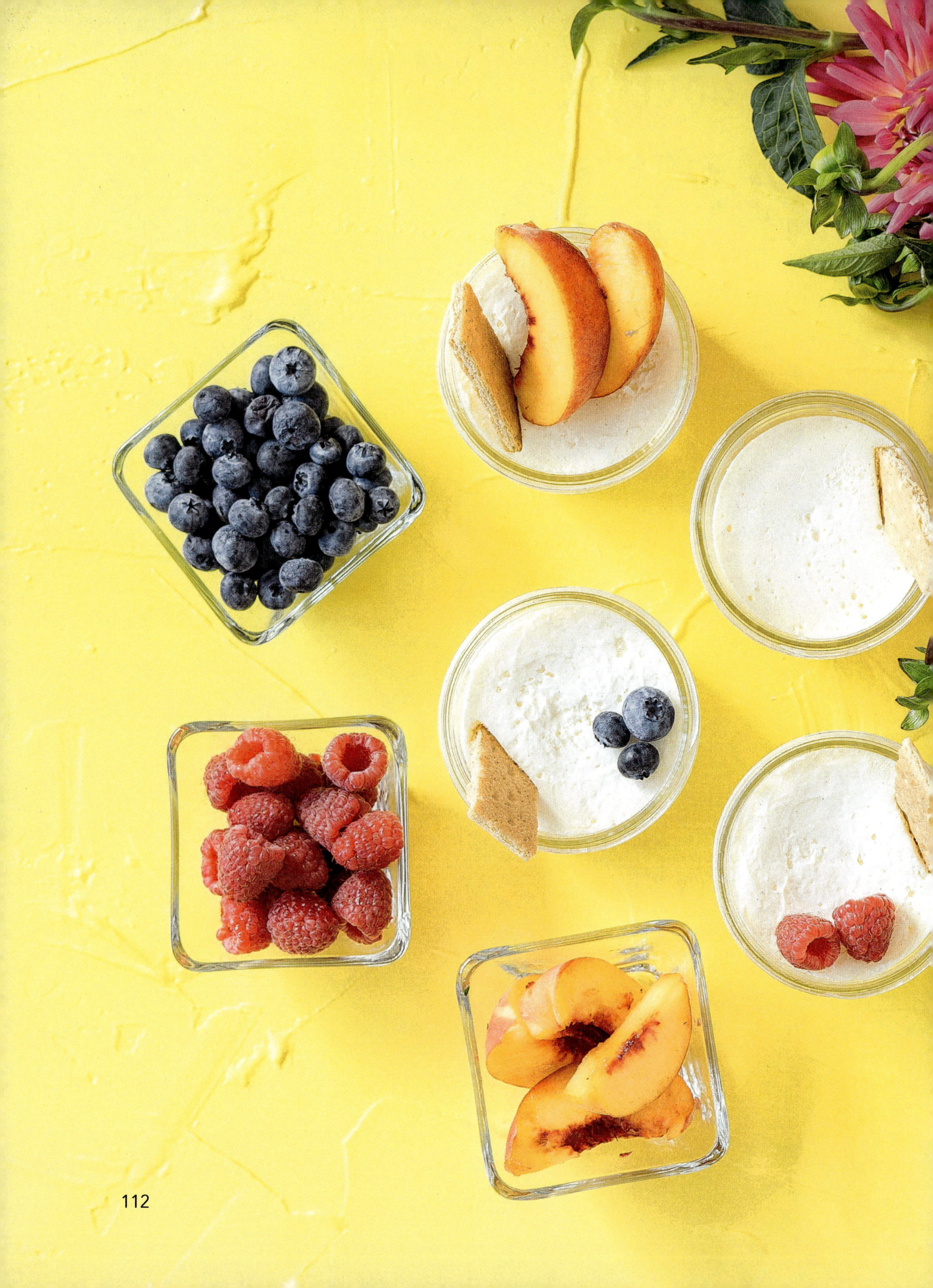

Desserts

Turn your Pinterest dessert fails into sous vide WINS. These little jars are about to up your dinner party game. They've slowly but surely become one of my favorite things to cook, especially when I'm feeding a group. They're ready-made in individual portions and, even better, they're forgiving.

Have you ever made creme brulée before this book? If you have, then you know how annoying it is. Here's what goes into it: bringing milk to just the right temperature before slowly and oh-so-carefully adding the eggs, and if you mess it up, you've got some super soupy scrambled eggs on your hands. Let's be real: it's a pain in the ass. And cheesecake and flourless chocolate cake ain't cakewalks either (#sorrynotsorry). Until now.

Throw your ingredients in a blender. Pour the mixture into jars. Drop them into a water bath. Serve. That's it. FOR REALS.

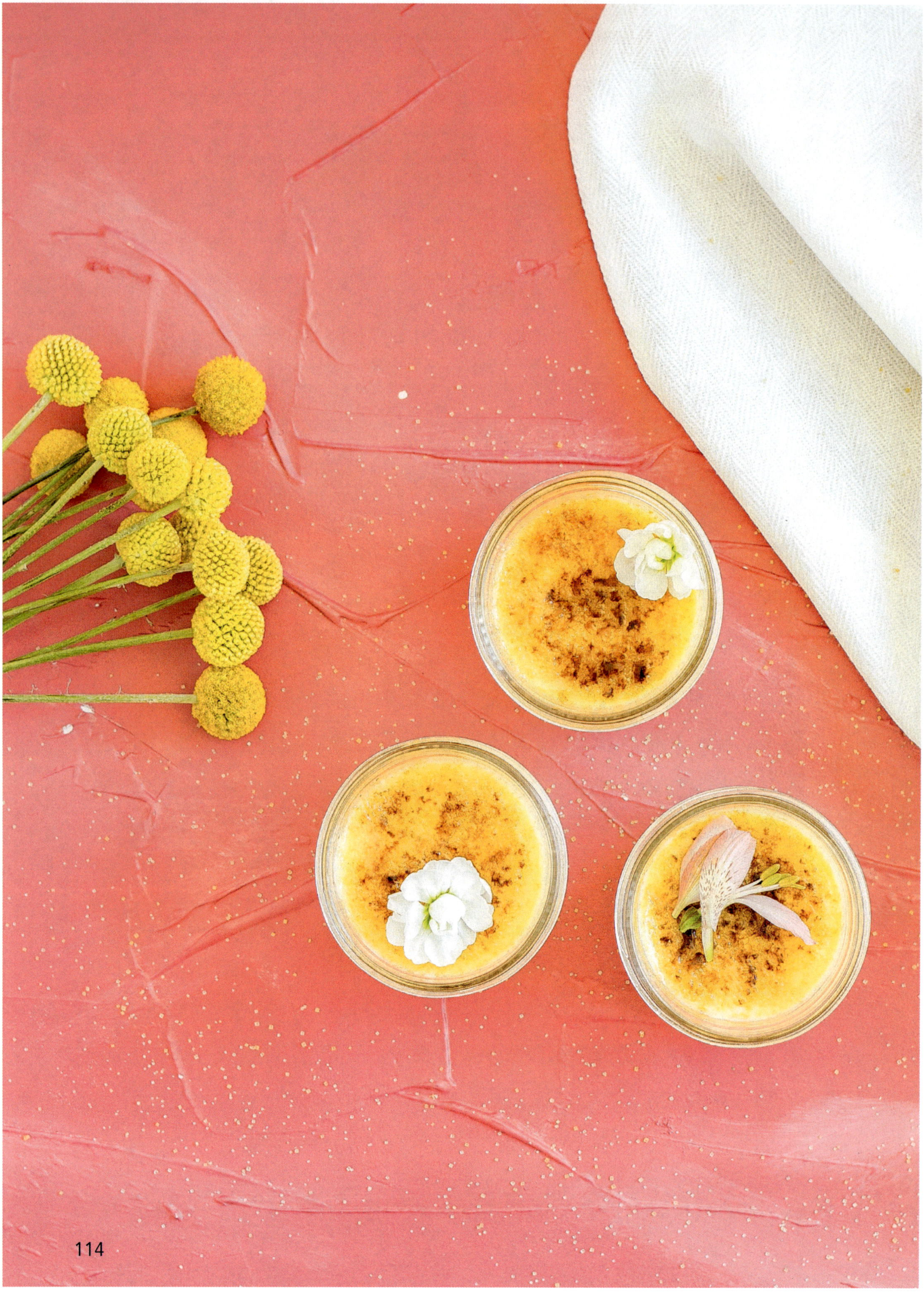

CREME BRULÉE

Creme brulée was my favorite dessert as a kid. I've always been a big fan of caramel/toffee flavors, not to mention mixing smooth and crunchy textures, so this dessert was a winner in my book right off the bat. At 12, I started attempting to recreate it at home but it was never the same. If only 12 year old me had known about sous vide cooking.

6 Servings

Ingredients
11 large egg yolks
Scant ½ cup granulated sugar
¼ tsp salt
2 ½ cups heavy cream
1 tsp vanilla extract
Turbinado sugar

Directions
1. Get immersion circulator setup and start preheating water bath to 175 degrees F. This is a hot temperature for sous vide cooking: don't forget to place a trivet under your container!
2. Arrange 6 half pint sized mason jars with lids in good condition, lids off.
3. Whisk together all ingredients except the turbinado sugar. Mix until no solid parts of the yolk are visible.
4. Evenly distribute the mixture between the six jars. Let sit until water is preheated to let bubbles on the top dissipate.
5. Place the undamaged lids on your jars. Close to "finger tight" (you should be able to easily unscrew with just your fingertips). Drop jars carefully into water. Jars should be completely submerged and you should see small air bubbles escaping the jars. If the jars are floating, your lid is on too tight.
7. Let cook for 1 hour. Remove mason jars to a towel on the counter to cool. Once cool to the touch, place in the refrigerator if not serving immediately. If serving immediately, place in an ice bath to continue cooling.
8. When ready to serve, remove the lids. Spoon turbinado sugar on the top of each custard to create a thin, even layer. 9. Use a small blow torch to caramelize the sugar. Serve.

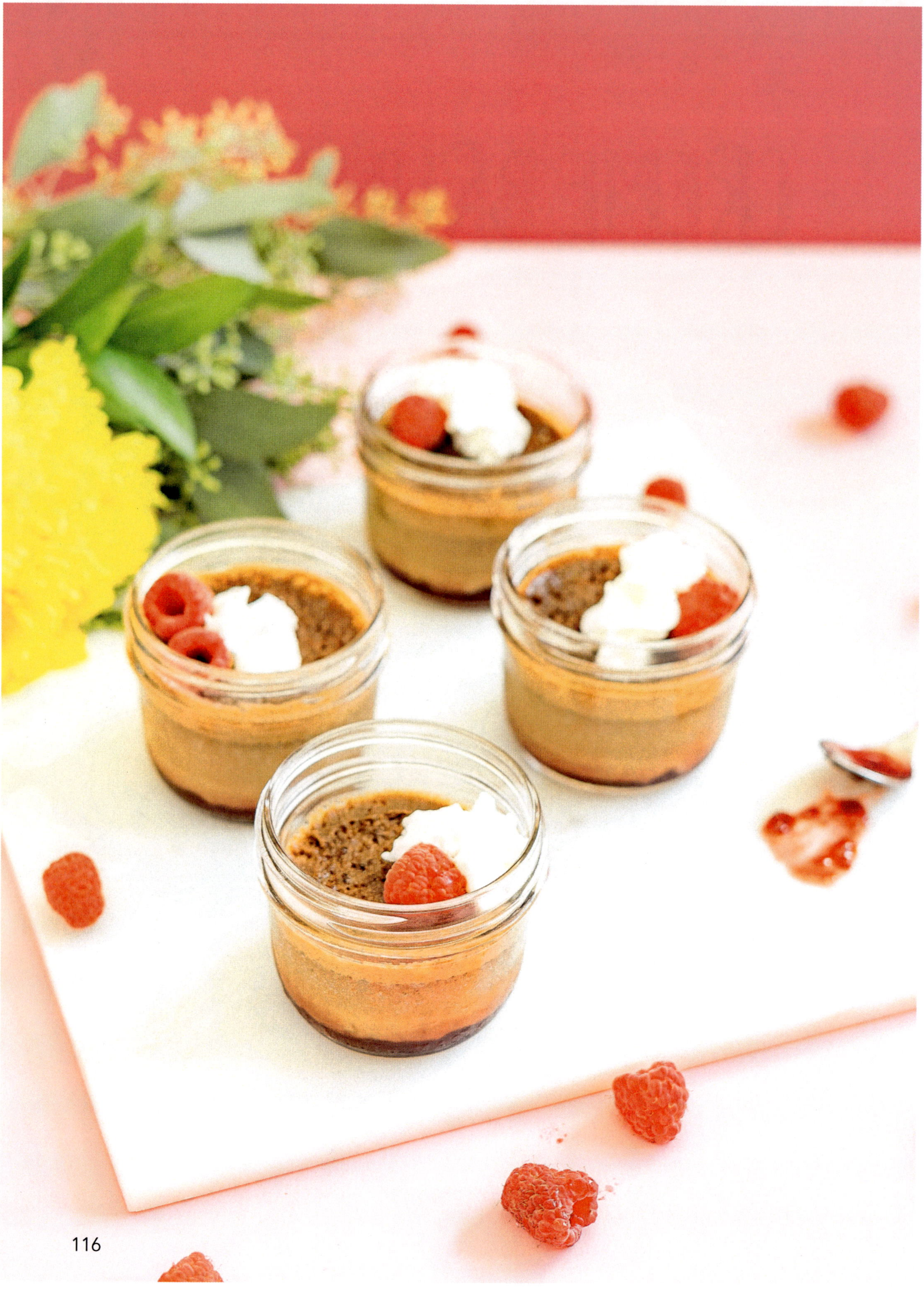

Flourless CHOCOLATE CAKE

When we talk decadent desserts, flourless chocolate cake is the be all, end all. It's rich and smooth (insert horrifying "how I like my men" joke here), and it's exactly what I'm looking for when I need a chocolate fix. I like to cut the decadence with a little raspberry jam, but you do you, friend.

4 Servings

Ingredients
4 large eggs, room temperature
½ pound chocolate of choice (semisweet or dark)
½ cup heavy cream, room temperature
½ cup butter
Raspberry jam (optional)
Whipped cream, for serving

Directions
1. Get immersion circulator setup and start preheating water bath to 115 degrees F.
2. Place chocolate and butter in your bag of choice and place in the water bath for 15 minutes to melt. Massage the bag every few minutes to blend the mixture.
3. Remove the bag and set the immersion circulator to 170 degrees F. This is a hot temperature for sous vide cooking: don't forget to place a trivet under your container!
4. Prepare 4 half pint sized, wide mouth mason jars by removing the lids and spraying the insides with nonstick cooking spray.
5. Beat the eggs in the bowl of a standing mixer at high speed until the volume of the eggs doubles.
7. Turn the mixer on low and add the heavy cream slowly. Cut a corner off the freezer bag and drizzle the melted chocolate mixture in slowly until the mixture is totally homogeneous.
8. If using, spoon a thin layer (about ¼ inch thick) of raspberry jam into the bottom of the jars.
9. Pour the batter evenly between the jars and tap the jars firmly on the palm of your hand to remove any air.
10. Place the undamaged lids on your jars. Close to "finger tight" (you should be able to easily unscrew with just your fingertips). Drop jars carefully into water. Jars should be completely submerged and you should see small air bubbles escaping the jars. If the jars are floating, your lid is on too tight.
11. Let cook for 1 hour. Remove mason jars to a towel on the counter to cool. Once cool to the touch, place in the refrigerator to chill for at least 8 hours.
12. Serve with whipped cream on top.

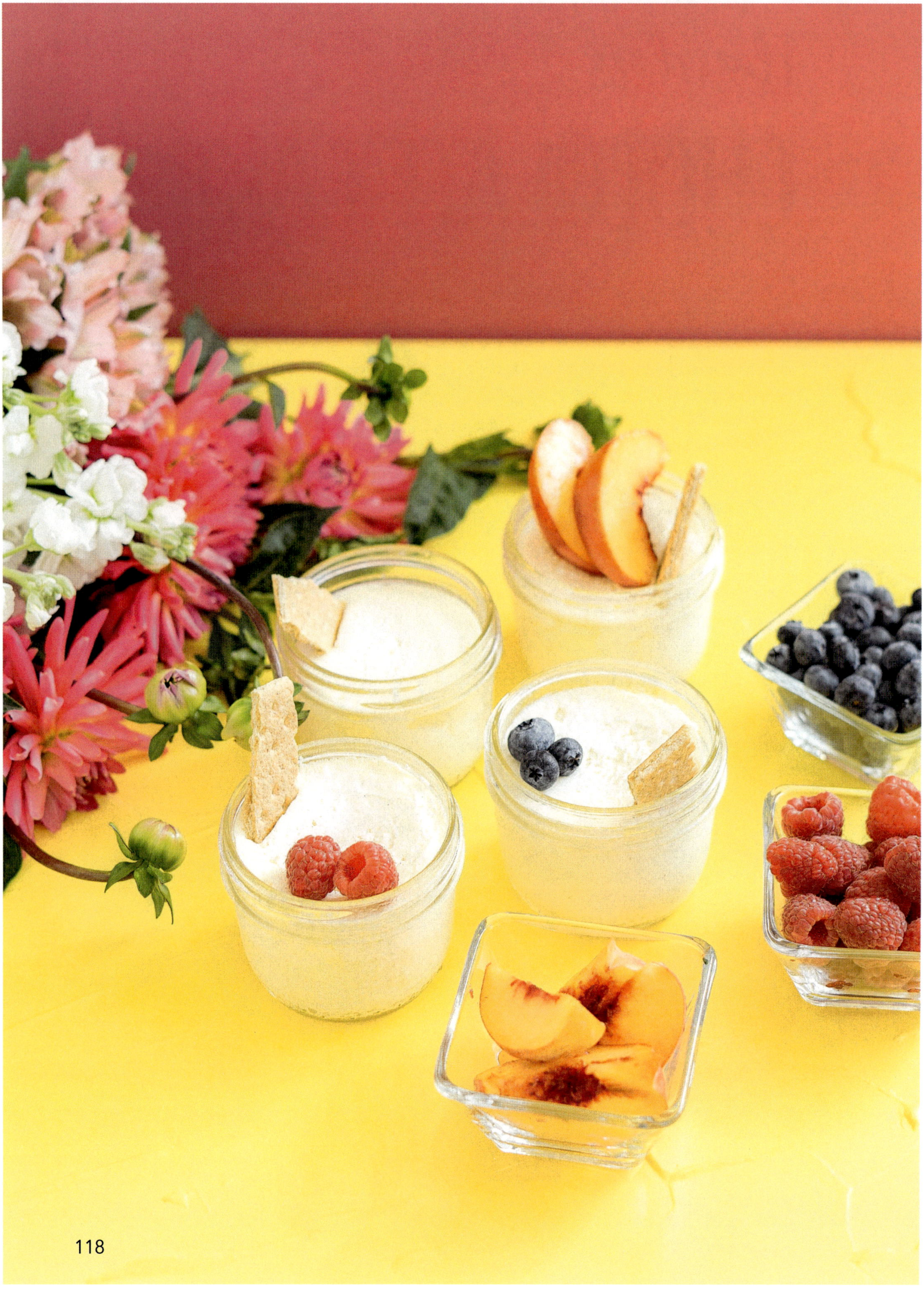

CHEESECAKE

Cheesecake has to be a universal favorite. Somehow, ice cream cake snuck it's way in as the go-to "fun" dessert for celebrations, but I call bull. Going forward, the dessert of choice will be cheesecake if I have anything to do with it. I mean, have you ever met someone who doesn't like cheesecake? Okay, don't answer that.

6 Servings

Ingredients
2 eight-ounce packages of cream cheese, softened
½ cup granulated sugar
¼ tsp salt
3 large eggs
1 tsp vanilla extract
½ cup heavy whipping cream

Directions
1. Get immersion circulator setup and start preheating water bath to 175 degrees F. This is a hot temperature for sous vide cooking: don't forget to place a trivet under your container!
2. Add all ingredients to a blender. Blend until smooth - there should be no cream cheese chunks and eggs should be completely incorporated. You may need to pause the blender and use a spatula to scrape down the sides a few times.
3. Prepare 6 half pint sized, wide mouth mason jars by removing the lids and spraying inside of jars with nonstick spray.
4. Pour the cream cheese mixture evenly between the jars.
5. Place the undamaged lids on your jars. Close to "finger tight" (you should be able to easily unscrew with just your fingertips). Drop jars carefully into water. Jars should be completely submerged and you should see small air bubbles escaping the jars. If the jars are floating, your lid is on too tight.
6. Let cook for 1 hour 30 mins. Remove mason jars to a towel on the counter to cool. Once cool to the touch, place in the refrigerator to chill overnight.
7. Serve with fruit, jam, or crumbled graham crackers if desired.

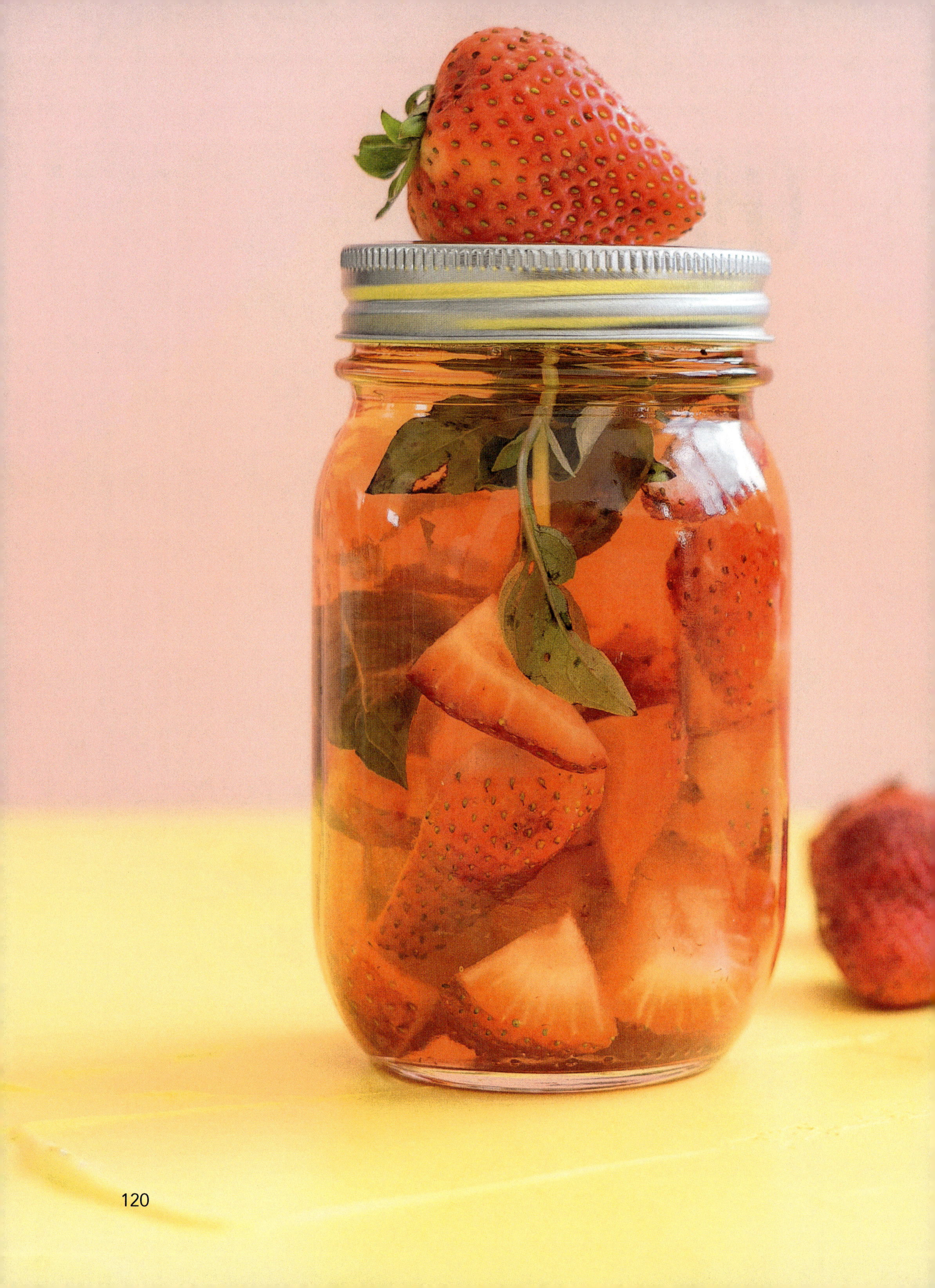

Liquor Infusions

I'm an alcohol girl. I don't know a better way to say that. I don't mean I drink a lot - I mean I like all the alcohol. Beer was my first love in college while living in Eugene, one of Oregon's best beer towns. Wine was my second: we fell in love when I moved to Cape Town, South Africa and spent many an afternoon at vineyards in Stellenbosch. Gin was the first liquor I really bonded with, followed by whisky and its friends bourbon and scotch. And who doesn't like rum, vodka, and tequila?

All this to say, you can't make me choose a favorite way to imbine, but I love playing bartender. Chalk it up to my years managing a restaurant or my love of cooking, but it's super fun to create boozy brainchildren.

So, when I read about sous vide liquor infusions, I had to get in on that. Why bother with sous vide for liquor infusions, you ask? Heat reduces time. Ordinarily, you can't use heat to speed up the infusion when it comes to alcohol because heat also means evaporation. But since the liquor stays in a sealed mason jar, this isn't a problem.

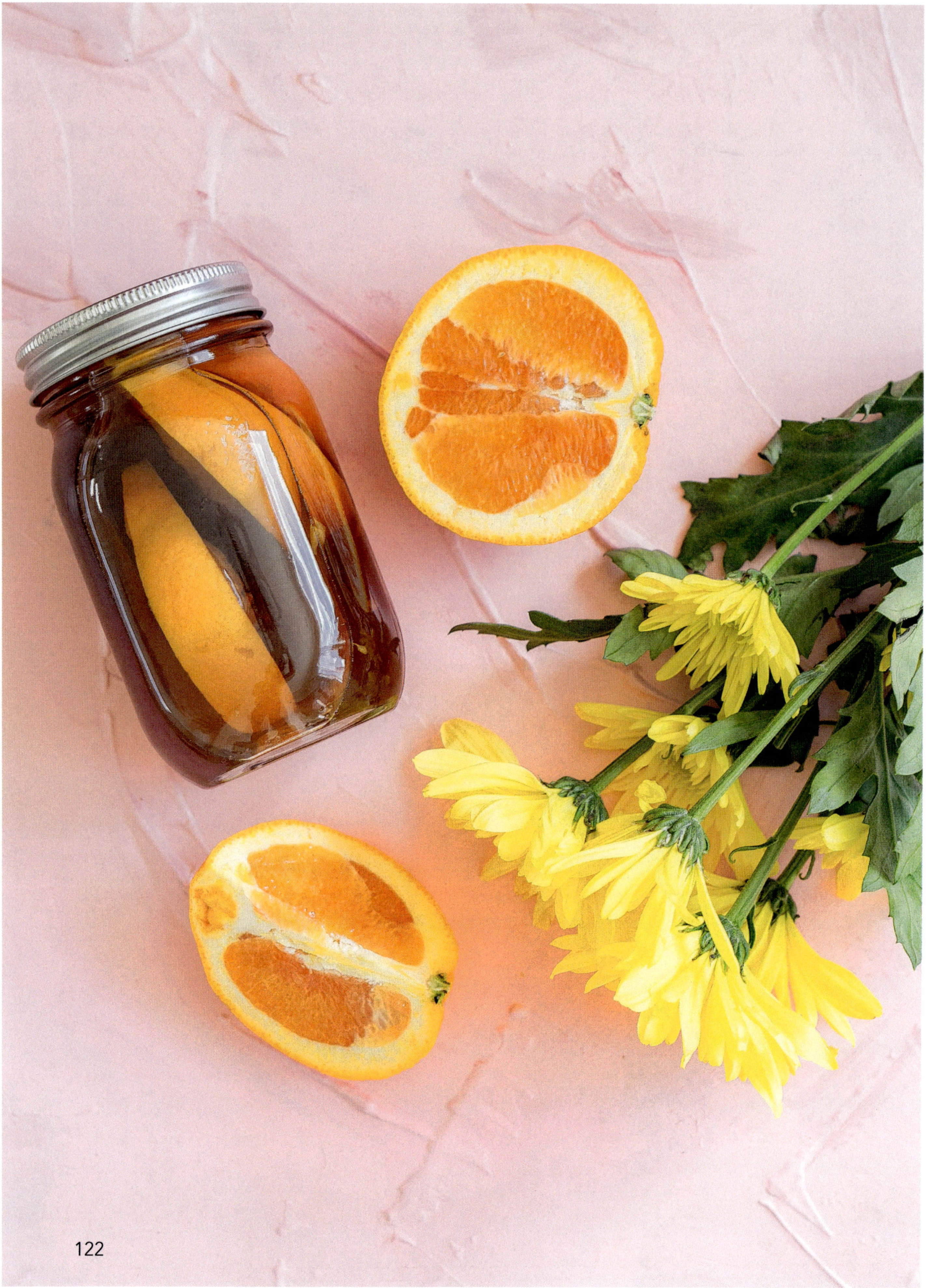

Cinnamon Orange INFUSED BOURBON

Meet your cold, January evening in front of the fire drink. Ideally it's snowing outside. You're bundled in a fleece blanket. You're watching a movie you've seen a thousand times over, or reading a book you've dog-eared time and again. And with this drink in your hand, you're warm and veering between tipsy and drunk. You're welcome. Drink it straight, or splash some hot apple cider over it.

Ingredients
1 cup bourbon
1 orange, cut into slices
2 cinnamon sticks

Directions
1. Get immersion circulator setup and start preheating water bath to 155 degrees F.
2. Add all ingredients to a pint-sized jar.
3. Place the undamaged lids on your jar. Close to "finger tight" (you should be able to easily unscrew with just your fingertips).
4. Shake to combine all ingredients. Drop jar carefully into water. Jar should be completely submerged and you should see small air bubbles escaping. If the jar is floating, your lid is on too tight.
5. Cook for at least 1 hour, up to 3 hours.
6. Remove from water bath and place on a towel and let cool for 30 minutes. Strain the liquid. Pour the liquid back into the jar and place in the fridge to store.

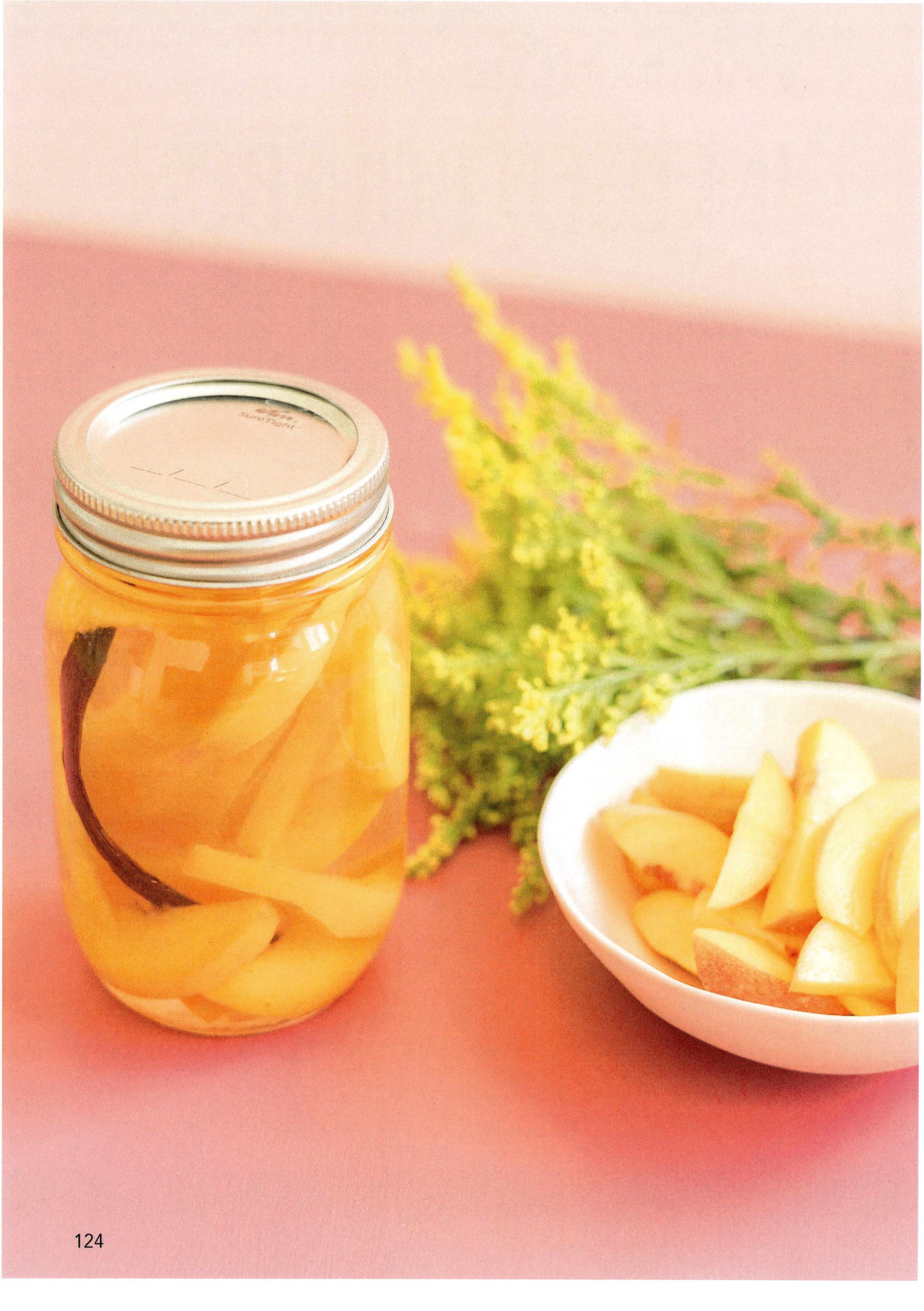
SureTight

Peach Vanilla VODKA

This is not your high-schooler-trying-to-buy-booze vanilla vodka. This is I-paid-$10-for-one-damn-vanilla-bean-and-threw-in-a-peach-'cause-I'm-fancy vodka. Are we clear? There are lots of mixer options with this one. Try pineapple juice and mint, sangria, or keep it simple and top it off with Sprite.

Ingredients
1 cup vodka
1 peach, cut into slices
2 vanilla beans

Directions
1. Get immersion circulator setup and start preheating water bath to 155 degrees F.
2. Add all ingredients to a pint-sized jar.
3. Place the undamaged lids on your jar. Close to "finger tight" (you should be able to easily unscrew with just your fingertips).
4. Shake to combine all ingredients. Drop jar carefully into water. Jar should be completely submerged and you should see small air bubbles escaping. If the jar is floating, your lid is on too tight.
5. Cook for at least 1 hour, up to 3 hours.
6. Remove from water bath and place on a towel and let cool for 30 minutes. Strain the liquid. Pour the liquid back into the jar and place in the fridge to store.

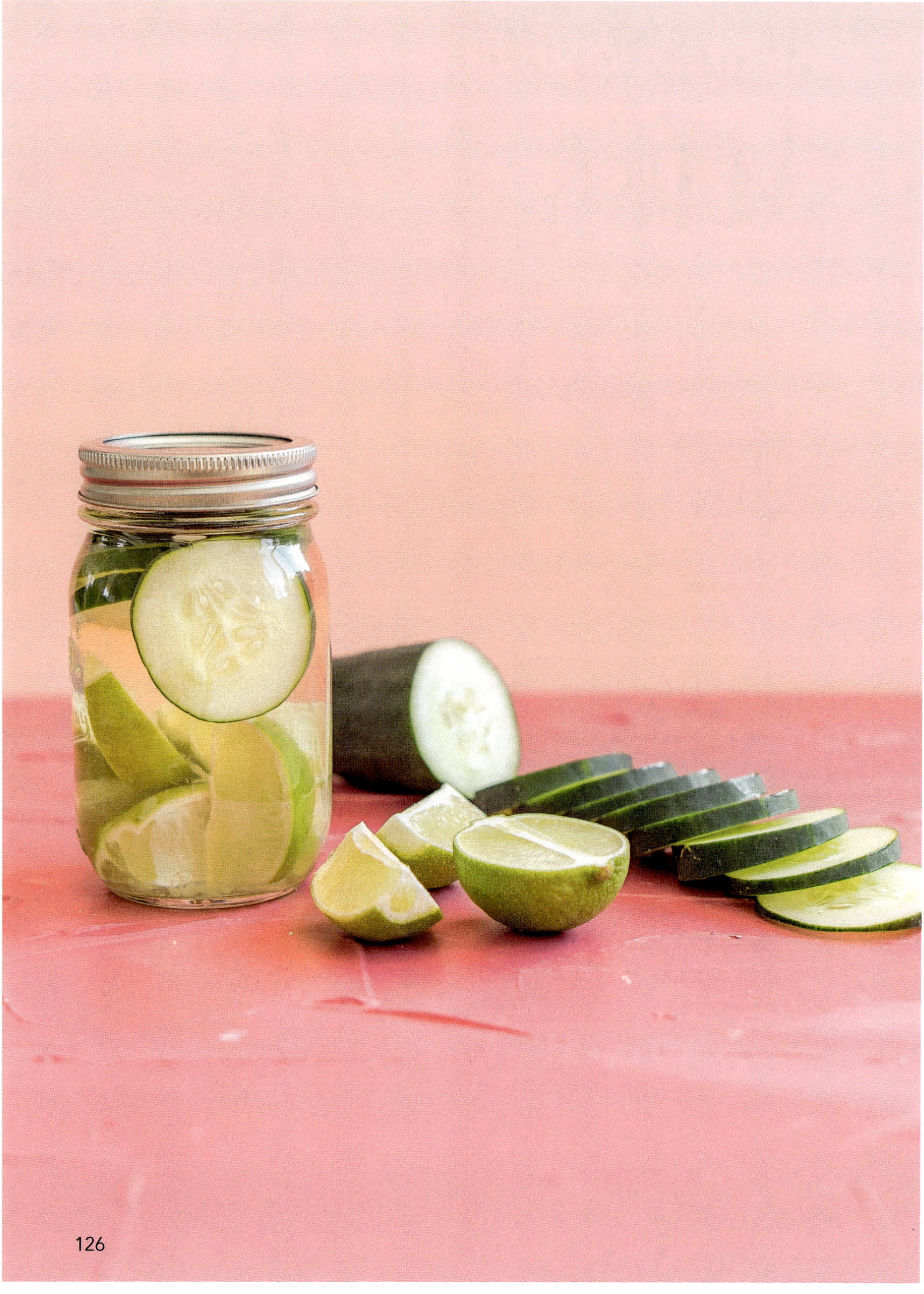

Cucumber Lime TEQUILA

This is your new go-to summer booze. It makes DIY margaritas way more fun, and it's just as good with my Husband and I's favorite mixer: Diet Squirt (do NOT pass judgement until you've imbibed). This classic pairing is all kinds of refreshing, and doing the infusion once means you don't have to pull out a long list of ingredients every time you want a fun cocktail.

Ingredients
1 cup tequila
2 limes, cut into slices
1/3 cup sliced cucumber

Directions
1. Get immersion circulator setup and start preheating water bath to 155 degrees F.
2. Add all ingredients to a pint-sized jar.
3. Place the undamaged lids on your jar. Close to "finger tight" (you should be able to easily unscrew with just your fingertips). Shake to combine all ingredients. Drop jar carefully into water. Jar should be completely submerged and you should see small air bubbles escaping. If the jar is floating, your lid is on too tight.
4. Cook for at least 1 hour, up to 3 hours.
5. Remove from water bath and place on a towel and let cool for 30 minutes. Strain the liquid. Pour the liquid back into the jar and place in the fridge to store.

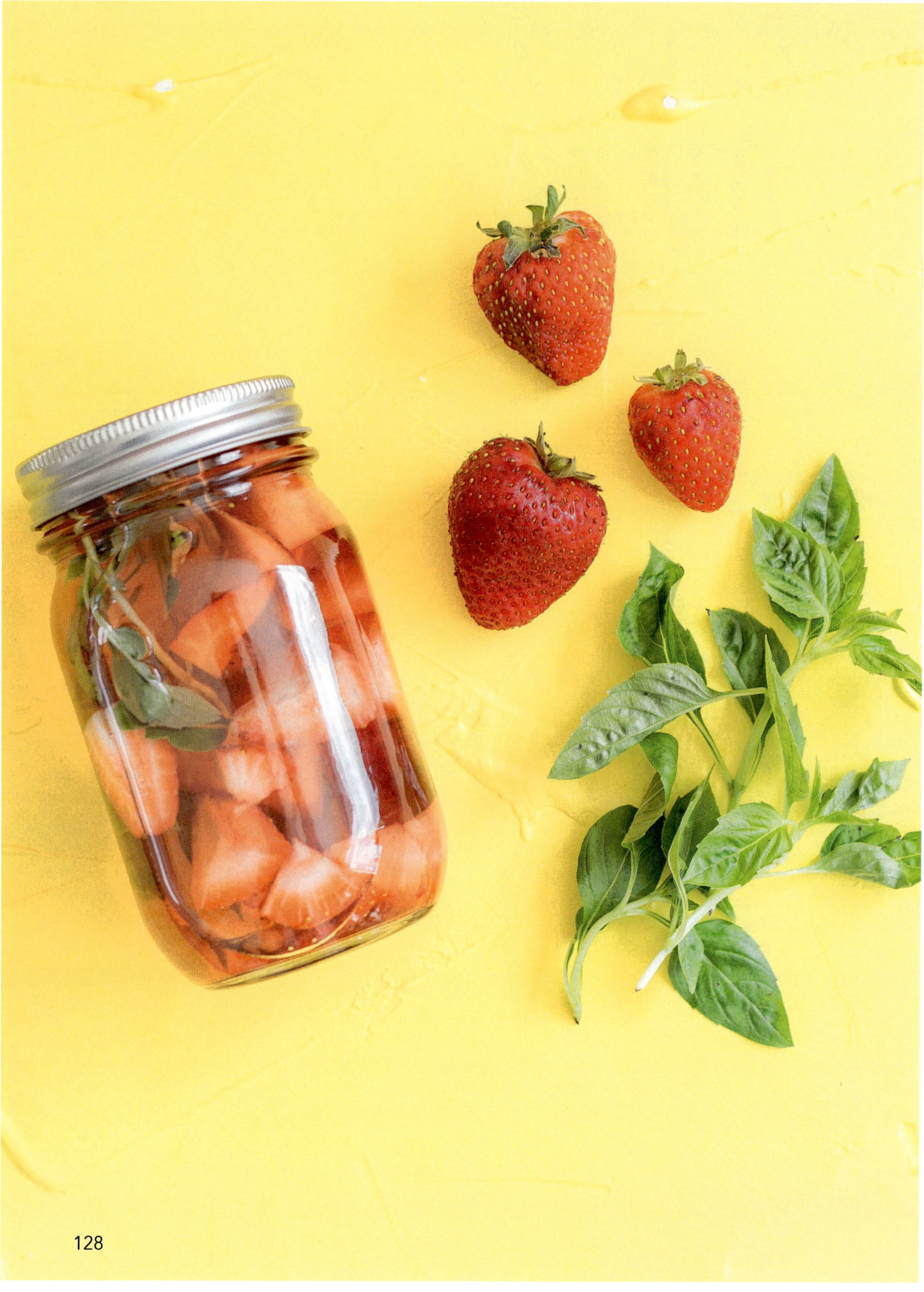

Strawberry Basil RUM

Strawberry basil is one of my favorite flavor combinations for beverages. It all goes back to a Strawberry Basil Lemonade served at a restaurant where I used to work. Strawberry is a usual customer, but basil - who she? Basil adds a fragrance that makes this infusion way more interesting. Mix it with LaCroix or use it in a mojito.

Ingredients
1 cup rum
½ cup chopped strawberries, hulled and tops removed
¼ cup roughly chopped basil leaves

Directions
1. Get immersion circulator setup and start preheating water bath to 155 degrees F.
2. Add all ingredients to a pint-sized jar.
3. Place the undamaged lids on your jar. Close to "finger tight" (you should be able to easily unscrew with just your fingertips).
4. Shake to combine all ingredients. Drop jar carefully into water. Jar should be completely submerged and you should see small air bubbles escaping. If the jar is floating, your lid is on too tight.
5. Drop the jars into the water bath. Cook for at least 1 hour, up to 3 hours.
6. Remove from water bath and place on a towel and let cool for 30 minutes. Strain the liquid. Pour the liquid back into the jar and place in the fridge to store.

ACKNOWLEDGMENTS

Carly. Graphic designer and photographer extraordinaire.

I'm grateful everyday that Carly and I became friends. It's rare in life to find someone whose passions line up so closely with your own. She is my go-to for nerding out on all things food, design, and photography. Not to mention, life in general. Even though my style is "distinctive" to say the least, she easily got my vision for this book and brought it to life. Thank you, thank you, thank you.

Dad.

I credit my "entrepreneurial spirit" to my dad. His "you'll never know until you try" approach to life has always inspired me. He instilled me with the confidence to go for anything I wanted from a young age, and I have. He's my voice of reason and encouragement. He has a faith in me that makes me have a faith in me.

Mom.

I am one of those lucky girls whose mom is truly her best friend. To know my mom is to love her. She is the kindest, most generous, hardworking, thoughtful, stylish, beautiful, fun… I could go on. And she's so reliably there for me. Without me even needing to ask, she offered to do anything and everything she could to help me accomplish this book. She was my sounding board, my photography assistant, and one of my editors. And I know she'll do it again when I think of my next all-consuming project.

My husband.

Eric, my husband, has been my cheerleader since we were 16 years old. There have been so many moments where I bit off more than I could chew and was plagued with self doubt. He stuck around and helped me push past those times to the other side, all with a smile on his face and a glass of wine for me in his hand. He's always made sure I saw my "big projects" through, from college to career changes and now, to this book.

He's eaten everything in this book. Multiple times. And patiently responded while I forced him to "be critical!" of each dish, over and over again. He didn't complain when I turned the second floor of our house into a home studio for 2 months while I shot this book. And now, he's letting me sous vide a turkey for Thanksgiving. Husband of the year.

Top right: Blake Miller (Chelsea's brother), Eric Cole (Chelsea's husband), and Gary Miller (Chelsea's Dad)
Middle right: Chelsea and her husband, Eric
Bottom: Chelsea and her mom, Laurie Miller
Top Left: Carly Jayne

INDEX

Bacon
- Bacon Blue Cheese Date Stuffed Burgers, 95
- Bacon Juicy Lucy, 101
- Cheddar, Bacon & Chive Egg Bites, 19
- Jalapeno Popper Stuffed Burgers, 97

Bacon Juicy Lucy, 101
Banana Almond Butter Overnight Oats, 27
Beef
- Bacon Blue Cheese Date Stuffed Burgers, 95
- Bacon Juicy Lucy, 101
- Beef Tataki, 61
- Caramelized Onion Pepper Jack Stuffed Burgers, 99
- Flank Steak, Korean, 55
- Flank Steak, Moroccan, 57
- Jalapeno Popper Stuffed Burgers, 97
- Ribeye, Umami, 59

Beef Tataki, 61
Blueberry Ginger Overnight Oats, 25
Burgers, Stuffed
- Bacon Juicy Lucy, 101
- Burgers, Bacon Blue Cheese Date, Stuffed, 95
- Burgers, Caramelized Onion Pepper Jack, Stuffed, 99
- Burgers, Jalapeno Popper, Stuffed, 97

Caramelized Onion & Brie Egg Bites, 17
Caramelized Onion Pepper Jack Stuffed Burgers, 99
Cheddar, Bacon & Chive Egg Bites, 19
Cheese
- Bacon Blue Cheese Date Stuffed Burgers, 95
- Bacon Juicy Lucy, 101
- Caramelized Onion & Brie Egg Bites, 17
- Caramelized Onion Pepper Jack Stuffed Burgers, 99
- Cheddar, Bacon & Chive Egg Bites, 19
- Cheesecake, 119
- Cilantro Lime Pesto Salmon, 75
- Cream Cheese and Chive Parsnips, 111
- Eggs & Lox, 21
- Greek White Fish, 85
- Jalapeno Popper Stuffed Burgers, 97
- Sun-Dried Tomato & Goat Cheese Egg Bites, 15

Cheesecake, 119
Chocolate Cake, Flourless, 117
Cinnamon Ginger Sweet Potatoes, 109
Cinnamon Orange Infused Bourbon, 123
Cilantro Lime Pesto Salmon, 75
Coconut
- Coconut Chai Overnight Oats, 31
- Thai Green Curry White Fish, 89

Coconut Chai Overnight Oats, 31
Coffee and Chili Rubbed Pork Chops, 45
Cream Cheese and Chive Parsnips, 111
Creamy Ginger Horseradish Salmon, 77
Creme Brulée, 115
Cucumber Lime Tequila, 127
Curried Butternut Squash, 107
Curry Spiced Pickled Carrots, 35
Desserts
- Cheesecake, 119
- Creme Brulée, 115
- Flourless Chocolate Cake, 117

Eggs
- Creme Brulée, 115
- Egg Bites, Caramelized Onion & Brie, 17
- Egg Bites, Cheddar, Bacon & Chive, 19
- Egg Bites, Sun-Dried Tomato & Goat Cheese 15
- Eggs & Lox, 21

Eggs & Lox, 21
Flourless Chocolate Cake, 117
Fruit
- Bacon Blue Cheese Date Stuffed Burgers, 95
- Banana Almond Butter Overnight Oats, 27
- Blueberry Ginger Overnight Oats, 25
- Cinnamon Orange Infused Bourbon, 123
- Harissa Orange Salmon, 79
- Peach and Thyme Pork Chops, Spicy, 49
- Peach Vanilla Vodka, 125
- Pomegranate Pickled Carrots, Spicy, 39
- Strawberry Balsamic Glazed Salmon, 81
- Strawberry Basil Rum, 129

Garlic Butter Poached Shrimp, 71
Garlicky Mashed Potatoes, 105
Ghee
- Beef Tataki, 61
- Coffee and Chili Rubbed Pork Chops, 45
- Korean Flank Steak, 55
- Miso White Cod, 91
- Moroccan Flank Steak, 57
- Peach and Thyme Pork Chops, Spicy, 49
- Salsa Verde Pork Chops, 47
- Tomato Balsamic Pork Chops, 51
- Umami Ribeye, 59

Ginger
- Beef Tataki, 61
- Blueberry Ginger Overnight Oats, 25
- Cinnamon Ginger Sweet Potatoes, 109
- Curried Butternut Squash, 107
- Curry Spiced Pickled Carrots, 35
- Ginger Horseradish Salmon, Creamy, 77
- Ras El Hanout, 56
- Korean Flank Steak, 55

Gochujang
- Korean Flank Steak, 55

Greek White Fish, 85
Harissa, 78
Harissa Orange Salmon, 79
Honey Garlic Sriracha Shrimp, 67
Jalapeno Popper Stuffed Burgers, 97
Jerk Shrimp, 69
Korean Flank Steak, 55
Lemon Dijon White Fish, 87
Lemon Pickled Asparagus, 37
Liquid Smoke
- Smoky Mustard Sandwich Pickles, 41

Liquor Infusions
- Bourbon, Cinnamon Orange Infused, 123
- Rum, Strawberry Basil, 129
- Tequila, Cucumber Lime, 127
- Vodka, Peach Vanilla, 125

Maple Pecan Overnight Oats, 29
Mashed Roots
    Butternut Squash, Curried, 107
    Cinnamon Ginger Sweet Potatoes, 109
    Cream Cheese and Chive Parsnips, 111
    Mashed Potatoes, Garlicky, 105
Miso White Cod, 91
Mojo Shrimp, 65
Moroccan Flank Steak, 57
Mustard
    Curry Spiced Pickled Carrots, 35
    Lemon Dijon White Fish, 87
    Mustard Sandwich Pickles, Smoky, 41
Nuts
    Banana Almond Butter Overnight Oats, 27
    Cilantro Lime Pesto Salmon, 75
    Maple Pecan Overnight Oats, 29
Steel Cut Oats
    Overnight Oats, Banana Almond Butter, 27
    Overnight Oats, Blueberry Ginger, 25
    Overnight Oats, Coconut Chai, 31
    Overnight Oats, Maple Pecan, 29
Peach Vanilla Vodka, 125
Pickles
    Pickled Asparagus, Lemon, 37
    Pickled Carrots, Curry Spiced, 35
    Pickled Carrots, Spicy Pomegranate, 39
    Pickles, Smoky Mustard Sandwich, 41
Pork
    Pork Chops, Coffee and Chili Rubbed, 45
    Pork Chops, Salsa Verde, 47
    Pork Chops, Spicy Peach and Thyme, 49
    Pork Chops, Tomato Balsamic, 51
Ras El Hanout, 56
Salmon
    Eggs & Lox, 21
    Salmon, Cilantro Lime Pesto, 75
    Salmon, Creamy Ginger Horseradish, 77
    Salmon, Harissa Orange, 79
    Salmon, Strawberry Balsamic Glazed, 81
Salsa Verde Pork Chops, 47
Shrimp
    Shrimp, Garlic Butter Poached, 71
    Shrimp, Honey Garlic Sriracha, 67
    Shrimp, Jerk, 69
    Shrimp, Mojo, 65
Smoked Salmon
    Eggs & Lox, 21
Smoky Mustard Sandwich Pickles, 41
Soy Sauce
    Beef Tataki, 61
    Jerk Shrimp, 69
    Korean Flank Steak, 55
    Umami Ribeye, 59
Spicy
    Creamy Ginger Horseradish Salmon, 77
    Harissa, 78
    Harissa Orange Salmon, 79
    Honey Garlic Sriracha Shrimp, 67
    Jalapeno Popper Stuffed Burgers, 97
    Jerk Shrimp, 69
    Mojo Shrimp, 65
    Spicy Peach and Thyme Pork Chops, 49
    Spicy Pomegranate Pickled Carrots, 39
Spicy Peach and Thyme Pork Chops, 49
Spicy Pomegranate Pickled Carrots, 39
Sriracha
    Sriracha Shrimp, Honey Garlic, 67

Steak
    Beef Tataki, 61
    Flank Steak, Korean, 55
    Flank Steak, Moroccan, 57
    Ribeye, Umami, 59
Strawberry Balsamic Glazed Salmon, 81
Strawberry Basil Rum, 129
Sun-Dried Tomato
    Greek White Fish, 85
    Sun-Dried Tomato & Goat Cheese Egg Bites, 15
    Umami Ribeye, 59
Sun-Dried Tomato & Goat Cheese Egg Bites, 15
Thai Green Curry White Fish, 89
Tomato Balsamic Pork Chops, 51
Umami Ribeye, 59
Vegetables
    Asparagus, Lemon Pickled, 37
    Butternut Squash, Curried, 107
    Carrots, Curry Spiced Pickled, 35
    Carrots, Spicy Pomegranate Pickled, 39
    Cucumber Lime Tequila, 127
    Parsnips, Cream Cheese and Chive, 111
    Potatoes, Garlicky Mashed, 105
    Sweet Potatoes, Cinnamon Ginger, 109
    Sandwich Pickles, Smoky Mustard, 41
White Fish
    White Cod, Miso, 91
    White Fish, Greek, 85
    White Fish, Lemon Dijon, 87
    White Fish, Thai Green Curry, 89

Made in the USA
Las Vegas, NV
06 August 2021